When Persistence and Providence Joined Hands

When Persistence and Providence Joined Hands

One Cardiac Surgeon's Journey

Surendra K. Chawla, MD

When Persistence and Providence Joined Hands:
One Cardiac Surgeon's Journey

Havan Press
info@HavanPress.com
HavanPress.com

ISBNs:
979-8-9912418-0-9 (print)
979-8-9912418-1-6 (eBook)

Printed in the United States of America

Cover and Interior design: 1106 Design

This book is dedicated to my wife, Ranjana.
Since the day we married in 1971, she has been my
closest companion and confidante. While I worked late hours
at the hospital taking care of my patients, she was taking care
of our children, running our household and volunteering in
our community. She is the first person I go to for advice, and
over the decades she has built our circles of friends and
confidently led us around the world
on our travel adventures.

My story would not be complete without the life lessons
from my parents, Darya Datta and Parbati Chawla. I am
also forever grateful to my children, Sujit and Sarika, and
my beloved grandchildren, Calvin and Leela Rigby.

This book is also in honor of the thousands of patients who
trusted me to take care of them, and hundreds of members of
the cardiac surgical team. The Cardiac Center at St. Francis
Hospital and Medical Center has been much more
than a workplace; together we created a family.

Foreword

I t is a privilege and honor to write the foreword to my dear friend's Surendra's memoir.

This is the gripping story of a life shaped by hard work, single-minded persistence, and an unwavering focus on success—despite a childhood marked by hardship.

Among his colleagues, a few stood out as truly brilliant and he was one of them. I remember one day during my residency training when he called me with the desire to come to the United States. When I approached my program chairman about considering him for the training program, I was asked, "Is he as good as you?" My immediate response was, "No, he is better."

Like many of us foreign graduates, Surendra faced uncertainty, cultural adaptation and relentless work—but these challenges only strengthened his resolve. Upon completing our training, many of us thought we could finally take a breath, but the real challenges were just beginning.

We both realized that we have to work twice as hard to succeed in a different country, to which we adapted.

We have both dedicated our lives to building our surgical careers, Surendra in Hartford, Connecticut, and me in New York City. Our communication never wavered and we have been lifelong friends. We have spent decades traveling the world together (although Surendra never took a liking to skiing!). Our children grew up together like family, and we were both honored to attend their weddings and watch the next generation be born.

Reading this book, I am still amazed by the parallels in our lives, and I imagine so many others who followed in a similar path will feel the same way.

Manjit S. Bains, MD FRCS©
Min H. and Yu-Fan C. Kao Chair in Thoracic Cancer
Memorial Sloan Kettering Cancer Center, New York, NY

Contents

$\jmath\kern-0.3em\xi$

Chapter One

I do not know what day I was born. March 5, 1942, was the date assigned to my birth later when I was first registered at the local school. This was in Karol Bagh, a town in the Central District of Delhi, India—but I was born hundreds of kilometers away in Montgomery (now known as Sahiwal), a city in Punjab, Pakistan. When I was born, Pakistan did not exist. We lived in one, undivided India, Hindus and Muslims alike, as brothers and sisters.

On August 15, 1947, the dissolution of the British Raj in the Indian subcontinent led to the creation of two countries, what would later be known as the Partition of India. Much has been written about the Partition, and every story that came out of it is important and galvanizing in its own way. What all these histories have in common is that the sudden news that Muslims would need to relocate to the newly established Dominion of Pakistan, and Hindus would likewise need to move to the Dominion of India caused a great deal of panic, enmity and eventually bloodshed. The loss of my birth certificate during my family's hurried evacuation from the western side of the Partition is, in retrospect, one of the most inconsequential events of those days.

I was only five years old at the time, and my recollection of that period in history is necessarily confined to a few certain impactful moments. Nonetheless, I have been filled in on the important events that befell us by older members of my family, especially my elder brother Hari Kishan Chawla (HK) through his handwritten notes, my brother Manohar Lal Chawla through his published book, *Five Fs of My Life*, published by Pendown Press; and orally by my sister Satish. Among my earliest memories is one in particular that could only have been guided by Providence, the divine hand of fate you will hear a lot about in these pages.

My father, Darya Datta Chawla, was Hindu, but he had several close personal friends who were Muslim. That was the way it was in those days, and it is important to remember that. When my father opened his law practice, his first client was in fact a Muslim. This man had a lot of property, and since my father was an expert in matters of real estate, of course he took the case. There was no prejudice in my father's heart, and he became known as a fair and just man.

On the day the Partition was established, one of my father's Muslim friends came running with a warning for us to leave immediately. This man told my father that in the next town there was a gang of people with guns and clubs trying to kill all Hindus—and this group was coming toward our house!

"You must leave everything here," this good man told my family. "I will try to preserve it as best I can. But you have to get out to a new house for the next seven to ten days till things settle down." But within three days, it was obvious we had to get out of the country.

I do not have much recollection of the house we left, beside the fact that it was a large, multistoried structure with a veranda in the middle and enough cows to provide milk for the family. Can you imagine having to leave everything behind on the spur of the moment? Perhaps if you or someone you know has experienced a house fire you might know the experience I am relating here. Every family heirloom, every antique, every savored piece of history—all lost. We could only take as much as would fit in two metal trunks. My father also took his bicycle and a gun, to help protect his family.

That there was no time to collect our possessions was very painful, a fact brought home to me by the repeated mention by my family members of these two metal trunks. But the danger my father's friend had advised us about was real. Everywhere, men, women and children were being massacred indiscriminately on the streets, in their houses, and especially on the trains, which were the main mode of transportation for those forced into this diaspora, whether heading east to India or west to Pakistan.

How did it go from everyone living peacefully together to such a violent state of affairs, so quickly and so terribly? The only thing I can compare it to is a mass hysteria. One person was shot someplace, and the other side reacted. *These Muslims or Hindus are killing my family, we must kill some of their family,* the frenzied thinking went. I wouldn't say any of it was premeditated like an act of terrorism. This was just the sheer erosion of trust that led to tragedy after tragedy.

I was too young to remember the detailed instances, plus women and children were well protected by the elders. We carried one metal trunk and a second small one with daily food rations.

We believe that father had decided to go to India from Montgomery via Okara (since our elder brother MK was visiting our uncle in the area). From there we would continue on to Raiwind, Ferozepur and finally reach Delhi. Not so easy!

Our train's first stop was in Okara to retrieve my brother. Luckily my father noticed a familiar person at the station and instructed him to go to town and find MK. By the time he returned with MK, the train had already started moving away. As my brother ran toward us in shorts and no shoes, my father swung him up onto the train, and we were off.

We traveled together with our family of parents and six sibling (four under 10 years old) and with four more adults comprised of relatives and friends.

As we reached Raiwind there were dead bodies, dismembered body parts and blood all over the station and people were cleaning the platform with blood spilled over the railway tracks. Soon my father realized that we were alone at the station because the next train to India was in the morning. We were to spend the night at the railway station.

Most of the elders have passed away and it is hard to verify the details. Something prompted my father to go the other platform where another train was ready to depart for India via Lahore, Amritsar and Delhi. Under guidance of Providence, once we reached the platform, the train had already started to move and we could not catch that train. As my family learned later, no one reached Lahore alive.

We had just witnessed from our platform that many people had died from massive injuries where the previous train was cleaned. We went back to our platform station to spend a night at the railways station retiring room quarters. I was told that it was the most horrific stay at the station. There were hoodlums with machete and clubs on the crossover bridge, and only one other family at the station.

The stationmaster had closed his office for the day but by good fortune he was waiting around for a government official to arrive. He was a Muslim man who was kind and helpful. This man took us to his office for protection. He even gave us some tea and food, although my mother was very strict about us not eating or drinking anything in case it was poisoned. In retrospect, we needn't have worried—no one was prepared enough in those days to use poison as a way to kill. It was only the sheer, unadulterated violence we had to worry about, a fact that was brought home to me later by a visit from my mother's brother, who came to our house in New Delhi when I was ten or twelve years old. He showed me where his entire left forearm was chopped off during the days immediately following the Partition as he tried to shield himself from danger.

The retiring room had a large front room where all adults stayed on night duty to keep a watch, while women and us children stayed in the back room. The night was at least safe.

When the morning arrived to freshen up, the bathrooms were up in the front. Women and children went in the open spaces to relieve themselves which they could not do because some hoodlum started to chase them. One of our friend's wife was pregnant and needed to go to the bathroom frequently. My mother built a concoction in their small kitchen for her.

It was time to go to the platform where the elders kept a close watch while women and children were still in the room for protection. Finally, the train arrived. The doors and windows were sealed shut by the passengers already sitting in the compartment. But again, Providence saw to it that we would be safe. Someone had opened the window a crack to ask why the train had stopped. Seeing an opportunity, my father smashed the glass window hurting himself and went in, opened the door, and had all my family and relatives enter the compartment.

My father instructed the family to bring his bicycle to the train which he had a great liking. They strongly rejected the idea that if there is some trouble we were all in danger of getting killed. He let go of the bicycle and gave it to the train master. He did keep his rifle in the trunk.

It was Providence too, that protected us the rest of the way. A Gorkha regiment, segment of Indian Army, were returning to Ferozepur after completing their duty in Pakistan, had boarded the train, and when they heard our story, they promised to help us during the night. Did some entity assign them to watch over us?

At last, our train reached the Delhi railway station, where government officials from relief funds and volunteers were there to help. My father had no connection with anyone in Delhi. And yet, as if out of thin air, a Sikh gentleman recognized my father. He had come to the station to pick up his relatives, but none of them had been on the train. He offered to take us to his house until we found some other place to move into. There were seven million people living in Delhi at the time, and my father had never been there. Even so, we were safely provided for.

This was not the case for the unlucky Muslims left behind on the eastern side of the Partition. There was intense fighting going on in the street. One of my earliest memories is of being on the upper floor of the house the Sikh man took us to and seeing a man burned alive. He was shoved inside a car tire while gasoline was poured on him. My brain was not yet developed enough to receive the full impact of the trauma of what I was witnessing, but I will never forget the smell of burning flesh. I often reflect on the terrible tragedy of the Partition, for both sides, when we are all one human family. Later, as a doctor, I knew it for sure; once you cut through the skin of a person during surgery, everyone's blood and tissues are the same color.

Soon thereafter, we started the hunt for a house we could all live in. People were occupying the empty houses of Muslims in India, just as Muslims were occupying the houses of people who had fled Pakistan like us. The first thing my father bought was a bicycle for transportation. He rode his bicycle around the neighborhood to look for vacant abandoned houses owned by

Muslims. He finally found a large, two-storied house located at 757 Faiz Road. A Sikh gentleman occupied the back portion, while the larger front portion was split between our family and the family of another friend of our father's, Jai Prakash. This remained our permanent house for the next forty years. Eventually, the property was officially allotted to us by the government in exchange for the property we left behind in Pakistan.

My father was an important engine of making everything happen for us in those days, while my mother was the soul of the family. I will tell you more about both of them in the next chapter, but in this context, I will say that I always drew strength from my father. He worked hard to protect the family and my mother's religious faith. She believed that everything happens when it is supposed to happen. The gods have ways of doing things, and we were supposed to leave Pakistan when we did. She never grieved over what we left behind there—even though it was everything. Whatever is lost, is lost, she would tell us, and it is the future that lies before us.

Chapter Two

The upheaval caused by the Partition translated directly into our living situation at 757 Faiz Road. Put simply, the house was chaotic. Initially there were two families living there: our family of nine, with my father and mother, us six children, and my grandmother, along with Jai Prakash and his wife and their two children. Soon my father's younger brother joined us with his wife and three children. This meant that eighteen people resided in what was, in effect, only half a house (the Sikh gentleman who helped us still controlled the back portion)—and there was only one bathroom!

The bathroom was built in the style where people of the same sex could enter together; a row of toilet seats stretched along the wall with no privacy between them. That is how it was done in the old days when people had a different sense of modesty. Men, for example, would sit down to do their business, all the while discussing politics and the events of the day with each other.

Now that we had both men and women living in the house, we obviously couldn't use the bathroom as freely. Sometimes, six or seven stalls would go unused while the others waited outside. You can imagine the kinds of quarrels that arise when people cannot take care of their bodily needs. It could even rise to the level of anger.

More often, it was pettiness. At night, people would line up their washing bowls in a row to determine who could go to the bathroom first in the morning. It was not unheard of for someone to move their bowl ahead of someone else's when they thought no one was looking. Each room accommodated one to three cots in the wintertime. In the summertime, the women slept in the veranda inside, while the men's cots were lined up outside of the house by the side of the main road. If someone moved his cot one inch into the area of another man's territory, a spat would ensue. In brief, it was not an environment that fostered cordial relationships.

It wasn't that something was wrong with us; overcrowding has been known to have this effect on the human species. My father realized this fact early and had another bathroom constructed for our family. Eventually, the other families moved out, and then we could breathe far more easily. We still only had the front portion of the house (we would eventually take over the entire property), but at least now there were six rooms for nine people—far more manageable.

As I mentioned, both of my parents had major impacts on our family, in quite different and complementary ways. One way to illustrate who each of these individuals were at their core is to describe which part of the house they occupied most often.

The front two rooms of our house were my father's office for the practice of law. One was for him, and the second was for his two junior associates: my oldest brother, MK, and Chaudhry Saheb—who would become my future brother-in-law—as well as a typist.

How can I describe my father? In Pakistan, he had finished his LLB, or bachelor's degree in law, with top honors. He then had to build his practice not once but twice—before and after the Partition—in two different countries, eventually becoming elected as the president of the High Court Bar in India, considered to be a very prestigious position. He was the only one of four brothers who went to school, and he ended up having such prominent clients as Indira Gandhi, the prime minister at the time, and other dignitaries. Obviously, there must have been a long road to travel from one end of that arc to the other!

When I reflect deeply on how my father did it, the answer appears to be simple common sense: He was honest and worked very hard. And yet, it was the consistent, disciplined repetition of a regular routine that contributed to his great success. He got up early in the morning for a walk, followed by a set of yoga exercises. He then ate a breakfast specially prepared by my mother, took a packed lunch from home with him to his rounds at court, and finally came home in the evening for a rest and some tea. But his day wouldn't stop there. He would then return to his home office to greet his clients and prepare their cases for the following day. It might have been nine or ten o'clock before he was truly finished for the day and able to have his dinner.

This schedule may paint my father as a workaholic, and yes, the hours were grueling. But he put in those hours both for his family—nothing was guaranteed in those days financially, far from it—and for his clients. He could not sleep unless he was fully prepared for the next day, a habit of his I picked up many years later when I became a surgeon. The night before every operation, I would refresh my memory as to the details of the case. Even if, like my father, I had done thousands of similar cases before, I would go through each step in my mind. That way, if something untoward happened and I was faced with a problem on the operating table, I would have more brain power available to respond appropriately in the moment. I could innovate, knowing that what could have been expected had already been thoroughly prepared for.

My father did not have enough time left over in his days to play with us children or to do things like take us to the movies. His main aim was to give all of his children an education, and to teach all my brothers and sisters to keep away from bad company or bad habits. My father wanted all of us to get at least a college degree, and he urged us to go beyond even that.

I remember him telling us this many times: "I do not have much wealth that I can divide. I can, however, provide you with an education. Knowledge is that which you can keep with you, which nobody can steal, and which will grow with you." These words did in fact prove strong enough for us to study hard and try to succeed. My eldest brother, MK, for example, the one who studied law, rose to become a judge of the High Court. He became a father figure to us all after our father's death, and a uniter of the family. Unfortunately, he succumbed to an acute hemorrhagic necrotizing pancreatitis and died before his time.

But all my siblings were similarly inspired. My father said he was going to pay for our education—and made good on that promise—and advised us that everyone should have a stable job. But he never said to his children, *you should do this and you should do that.* He left it to us to find the path best suited for us.

I believe my path first revealed itself to me the day one of my mother's sisters came for a visit. When my mother inquired about the health of another relative of ours, my aunt replied that this person had gone to the hospital where they had opened her belly . . . and she had died. I was only nine or ten at the time, but I remember asking my mother, "How come she went to the hospital and she died? Isn't that the place where you are supposed to get better, to heal and then come home?" I had not yet chosen premedical as my educational route; I was just a curious boy feeling the first stirrings of my passion for medicine.

Speaking of my mother, Parbati Devi Chawla, she was the most likely source I would go to when confronted with some of the big questions of life like this. I could usually find her in her part of the house, which included a small prayer room. She would be in there very early in the morning, well before six on most days, praying to Rama and Krishna, the main Hindu gods that she revered—this from a cast of a hundred divinities or more in our religion that embodied health, wealth, fire, water, rain, and so forth.

After that, she would get breakfast ready for the whole family with the help of a servant, including the food my father would take in a tiffin carrier for his lunch at court. She would repeat a similar set of actions in the evening, preparing my father's tea and dinner for everyone at the time they wished to eat.

In between these activities, most of my mother's afternoons were spent in the main temple, reciting prayers with other devotees. My mother never learned to read or write either Hindi or English, and yet she didn't need literacy to have a deep understanding of the world. In fact, she was the gentlest, most God-loving person I have ever met.

She believed in destiny and would take advice from her priest to keep her family safe and healthy. "What happens, we have to accept it," she would tell me. "Whatever is in your destiny will happen and you cannot change it. If you try to achieve something very strenuously and do not get it, it is because God did not want you to get it." She would continually remind me that God has sent all of us into this world with a purpose. And that I shouldn't waste my time doing things that were meant for someone else to do. Her faith was a faith put into action.

The main goal in this life, according to my mother, is to be a good person and try to attain Moksha, where you become part of the Almighty and do not have to continually follow the circle of birth and rebirth. Her devotion to and belief in the Almighty meant for her that your soul never dies—it merely changes its outer garb and reemerges. You could be reborn as any living being, whether human or not; she believed that God existed in all living beings.

To illustrate a message like that, my mother would often tell simple stories that have stayed with me my entire life, such as this one: A person wanted to kill a bird but did not want anyone to see him doing this. Therefore, he went to the corner of the darkest room in the house with the bird and his knife. At the moment he was about to kill, he realized that God was in this bird also. And not only that, but God was watching him. He could not then kill the bird. That story came back to me many times in my medical practice when I realized while performing open heart surgery on my patients that I was operating on God in human form. I could not afford to take shortcuts or leave anything imperfect on the operating table, not at least as far as was within my human capability.

I did not read religious books growing up, as I likely should have done. I believed it was more important to study the books that belonged to my curriculum at school so I could pass various examinations. Fortunately for me, I had my mother's stories to help guide me in my paths of this world. For example, she believed that one should not lie unless it was for the benefit of others. She illustrated this concept by telling the story of a Muslim who was running after a cow to kill her. At a fork in the road, he asked someone, "Have you seen a cow? Which road has she gone down?" This person thought, *If I tell the truth he will certainly kill the cow, but if I lie, the cow's life can be spared.* He then instructed the Muslim person to go the wrong way.

My mother taught me so many things. I won't tell you all of the stories in which her messages were embodied, but I do want to pass along the code that she gave to me. This included the following tenets:

> *Serve others; do not wait for the results. Give food to the hungry, and God will give you more.*

> *Stay within your means; our family did not have enough, but we did not borrow money.*

> *Love your enemy as well as your friends.*

> *Every person is good. Some are ten percent good and some are ninety percent good. Look for their good side.*

> *If someone is evil, they will be paid back, either in this life or the next.*

> *Look at the forceful stream of water when it meets a big rock and cannot go any further. The force of the water does not just sit there—it goes around the rock and finds a different path. This is applicable in everyday life.*

> *Do not compare yourself to anyone who has more, but be thankful that you have more than many who have none.*

> *Respect your elders because they have been sent ahead earlier to help you.*

I found this last one had wide application in my life, but it certainly applies most to my father and my mother, the two main characters of this chapter.

⚡

Chapter Three

Many of the memories from my earliest years are little more than impressions, yet it seems to me that everything I remember, I remember for a reason. My aptitudes (and drawbacks!) in school, my relationship with my family, these were all formative experiences that made me the man I became. Or perhaps the man I was destined to become went through these events in a particular way, thus already showing the character and temperament I possessed. Who is to say? I just know that when I look back at certain childhood stories, I see they had a direct bearing on me later in life, and I marvel at that fact.

The first school I attended, from the age of five, was the Dayanand Anglo Vedic (DAV) Higher Secondary School. Established in 1933, it was all male, and it was located on Chitra Gupta Road, in Paharganj, New Delhi. It was only about a mile from our house, so I would walk both ways every day unless there were heavy rains. In that case, my father would send his car and driver to pick me up from school. The weather could be quite extreme in Delhi. Sometimes, on particularly hot days, the high could hit over 120°F. Any time it was over 100°F, my mother would send me to school in a horse-drawn vehicle known as a tonga, and she would buy me a pack of sugarcane cubes and a wet towel to cover my head so I could avoid heatstroke.

The temperature was not the only thing that could make me dizzy in those days, however. I also felt quite unsteady any time I had to do any public speaking. I don't know if this fear also affects you, but I understand it is a very common phobia, as common as the fear of snakes or needles or flying. Each morning at school, a different student would stand on a platform to lead the prayers. I was very shy to begin with, and having to go up in front of the whole school was nearly unbearable for me. This fear continued throughout my life, even in my career, and I was never able to discover the reason for it. I could be quite eloquent when speaking one-on-one with someone and would often be able to convince them of my point of view. But whether there were ten people or a hundred present, as in some of my later medical presentations, I would forget the next sentence unless everything was tightly scripted and laid out before me.

I didn't make many missteps when I was young, but there were the inevitable errors of judgment that all children make. One time at school, I was caught stealing a few petty items such as toothpaste in an outdoor open market; our headmaster gave me such a hard slap, I did not dare steal anything since! When it wasn't the headmaster enforcing the rules, it was my mother, as my father had to work so often.

Around the age of ten, I used to sneak out in the hot, bright sun with my friends and play Gulli Danda and Kanche. Part of our play was to engage in some betting when I thought my mother was resting. When she found out, she pulled me by my ears and dragged me home in front of my friends. It was truly a mortifying scene!

On the way home she said to me, "You should not play and gamble with these children. Their fathers have no jobs, they simply sleep all day, with no ambitions and no achievements. If you want to be one of them, be my guest. But if you don't, all you have to do is look at your father, who has worked so hard to get his law degree, to become a practicing lawyer who can support the entire family, and to top it all off, to earn the respect of society."

That voice has stuck in my head all these years as a reminder—and every time I hear it, I can still feel the pain in my earlobe from that day!

I would not have described my siblings as friends during this time, as I was the youngest child, and we did not have much in common. That situation would change later in life, when I became quite close to them. Nonetheless, all six siblings always got along. We may not have gotten together to see a movie, but not a single one of us ever shouted at one another. There was such harmony in our family, in fact, that other families were envious of our lack of infighting. They called it the "Chawla Khandan"—"Khan" meaning *family* and "Dan" meaning *together*, or the family ethos.

In our case, the normal relationships that might develop between brothers and sisters was interrupted, of course, by the trauma resulting from the Partition. After some years, things stabilized and the internal bonds began to rebuild—or build for the first time, as in my case. Throughout these pages, I will introduce my siblings and hopefully do them the justice they deserve, beginning with my two eldest brothers.

I always looked up to my eldest brother, MK. For example, as a young boy, I saw him grow a mustache and resolved I would do the same. I have had that mustache ever since—it is part of my "look." It was a big deal for me when MK first started inviting me to take a walk with him and his friends in Karol Bagh Park near our house. They had a routine of buying aloo and puri for their breakfast, but one day it was raining very heavily. I was so curious as to how my brother was going to be able to pay in that situation. Wouldn't the money get wet? When it came time to settle with the vendor, my brother bent down and reached for some dry rupee notes stashed inside his socks. I thought this was ingenious!

Having a brother like that was akin to having a second father. I had my first cup of coffee with MK while vacationing in Simla, a hill station in the North. Through his actions, he showed me how to think ahead and put into motion what you had learned. It could be something small, like knowing that the *halwai* (confectioner) who had the best fresh *burfi* (sweets) in Simla opened at seven in the morning and was going to sell out by nine—so you had better get there during that window if you didn't want to be disappointed!

MK also bought me my first sophisticated camera. He saw my aptitude for taking photographs and took me to Connaught Place in Delhi so I could learn about box cameras, lenses, and refractions. It benefitted him as well, as I would later take pictures of all our family members, especially his own newborn son, Prag, the first addition from the next generation to join our clan. Photography became an important tool for me later in my medical studies and practice, documenting various stages and varieties of anatomical operations. This was another one of those seeds that was planted in my childhood and later came to blossom in adult life. In my middle and older years, this passion of mine culminated in my becoming the designated photographer for my traveling companions and conceiving artistic shots of buildings, the ocean, sunsets, and portraits. These images are collected in many albums and boxes, waiting to be digitized for my descendants to enjoy.

One more word about MK before I leave him for the time being: He was always a voice of reason. This dates back to when he was just eighteen and was vacationing in Okara when the Partition occurred. I already told you about how he had to run for our train, and also about how my father had brought his gun. Well, on that trip, my father was threatening to kill any Pakistani who came near us, assuming these persons meant to do us harm. It was left to MK to talk some sense into my father. He and other family members managed to convince my father that even the noise of a single gunshot would result in all of us getting killed by the bad elements around the train station. This calmed my father down and was emblematic of

MK's ability to help make peace in any situation in the extended Chawla family.

While MK was a uniter, my brother Hari Kishan (HK) was a caretaker. Originally, HK chose the field of mathematics and statistics in which he excelled; he was instrumental in teaching many children in the family these subjects. His career started out in the private sector, but he then shifted to prestigious governmental service. As part of that role, he was given a house for his family at Moti Bagh, which was on the way to the airport. Whenever we visited India later, it was a custom to meet him on the way to our house. Yet, when our father got sick, HK thought nothing of coming back to the family house with his family to start taking care of our father.

One thing I remember about HK from my youth was when he joined the Rashtriya Swayamsevak Sangh, or RSS, an organization that was the right wing of the Congress party. It was founded by Keshav Baliram Hedgewar in 1925, as part of the movement against British rule and as a response to the rioting between Hindus and Muslims. It was a well-disciplined organization with a reputation for punctuality. It emphasized staying healthy with exercise and group games, presumably so Hindus could defend themselves but also as a way of upholding Hindu values.

I remember joining in these games, including one called Kabaddi. It is kind of like tackle tag, if you can imagine such a thing. The objective is for one player on offense to run into the opposing team's half of the court, touch as many players on the other team as they can and call them out, and return to our side—all without being tackled by defenders in a timespan while holding their breath.

One day during a game of Kabaddi, I was coming back to my own side when a member of the other team jumped on my right leg and broke my tibia. The break occurred in the lower third of the bone, but it was not properly set by the compounder (a role equivalent to a physical assistant today), so my leg remained shorter for the rest of my life. From that point on, I would always need an insert in one of my shoes to even out my gait.

Manohar Lal, my third brother, was six years older than me. He does not recollect this, but I remember one incident when he took me to a nearby *halwai* and, pointing at me, told the shopkeeper, "He is my younger brother. Give him a full glass of milk and all the *malai* (cream) on top." Nowadays, this would be unheard of because of high cholesterol levels! We were reunited when I was in the Chandigarh residency for a Master of Surgery.

Satish, my eldest sister, was the quietest, most thoughtful person during our childhood. She was the most helpful to all our siblings, especially to me. Even today, in our golden years, she addresses me as "Hi Bache," meaning "My Child." When our mother died, she gracefully took on the role of mother figure, carrying on all the religious functions and traditions for the family.

My other sister Ramesh is only a year older than I, and she has also excelled in the field of medicine. Our close age and shared interests have bonded us throughout our lives, and I will share more about her influences in the coming pages.

My parents were not trained in medicine, but they did have some lore passed down to them through the generations that I later came to appreciate as accurate in its own way. For example, while I was recovering from my broken leg, my mother insisted on taking me out in the sunshine for "my bones to heal faster." I later learned that some doctors recommend large supplements of Vitamin D and exposure to sunshine during periods of bone healing, so her advice was actually spot-on!

My father, too, would pass on healthful advice, such as when we took a walk in Gandhi Park. He would pat me on my back and say, "Keep your back straight; otherwise, it will be bent forever." This also turned out to be true. Some of my parents' medical advice I followed, of course, just to be respectful of the older generation. When my mother advised me to walk barefoot on fresh, rain-soaked grass because it would "help my brain," I figured it couldn't hurt, even though I still don't know what the science is behind that. After all, not everything medical needs to be seen on a scan or administered by an injection. Living well in the world by suiting yourself properly to your environment can also do your body a world of good.

Chapter Four

I have other memories from my childhood. I remember learning how to play tennis when I was younger. My father took me to his club one day and asked the tennis pro to teach me how to play—something that I became quite proficient at during medical school and continued to enjoy throughout my professional career. I also remember when I learned to drive. Growing up, we had a driver who would take my father to the high court and his office in Dariba Kalan, a notable bazaar in Delhi. We dared not ask our father for driving lessons, as he was too occupied with professional matters, and he likely considered the damage we might do to his vehicle as well. So I asked our driver to help me on the side, and he obliged. When my father was in his home office, our driver would keep the hood of the car raised and pretend to look around at something he might have just fixed.

He would then approach my father and say, "I think everything is OK now." (My father probably didn't even know anything was wrong in the first place—in large part because nothing was). Our driver would continue, "I am going for a test drive just to be sure. Chote Sahib (that was me) wants to go with me, is that OK?"

After our driver got permission to take me, we would drive to the isolated, less-trafficked Buddha Park near the airport, where he taught me how to use a stick shift. The automatic car had not yet arrived in India.

But most of the details I remember about my childhood center on my education. Whenever something had to do with science or mathematics, the material seemed to just come by itself—I knew I had it. Humanities proved more of a challenge, however. I liked English only a little bit, and history and geography less. How was I supposed to remember when certain Muslim rulers controlled our country, or in what order they had reigned? I invented an acronym system to help me with that, and in fact, acronyms and other mnemonic devices became an important part of my study habits going forward. If I could remember the acronym and put that down on the test paper, I had a much better chance of filling in each of the first letters with the required information.

For any classes we were truly struggling in, our teacher encouraged us to attend his house for private tutoring. Since everyone wanted to pass the examinations, most did attend, except for a few students who could not afford it. Two students in that latter category, Girish Gupta and Kamal Rattan, were among the brightest students in our class. I admired them and kept their company, while at the same time feeling grateful that my father worked so hard to make sure this additional tutoring was available to me. I lost touch with Girish, but Kamal went on to great success practicing orthopedic surgery in the U.S. before retiring to live in India in a farmhouse.

The support of my family once again came to the fore when I decided to go premedical at the age of sixteen. "Premedical" is the term given to the one year of intense studying you must do if you want to enter medical school. I spent my premedical year at Hans Raj College, which was about three miles from our house. Hans Raj was located in the neighborhood of Malka Ganj and was affiliated with the University of Delhi. I traveled to college on a bicycle wearing a *salwar kameez* pajama set with loose pants and a tunic on top; I did not yet own any formal shirts or trousers in 1958. There was no time to socialize or make friends in those days. We students would listen to lectures in the morning, then come home, and, after a rest, return to the textbook to make our notes. If one managed to pass the year-end examination with a high enough score to be in the First Class, that was a sure ticket to entering medical school, so the pressure was intense. And this was where my family came in.

As I said, my sister Ramesh also had an inclination toward medicine, and I was one year behind her. This gave me a big advantage because I got all her books. The cost was much less this way, of course, but even more than that, all the important parts were already underlined! It made studying these texts a very smooth process. One needed a score of 360 to be guaranteed a

First Class ranking. I maintain to this day that were it not for my sister's influence and handing down her study materials, I would not have succeeded the way I did.

Entrance to medical school should by then have been a pretty straightforward endeavor. I applied to several places, but I concentrated on the two medical schools in Delhi: Maulana Azad Medical College/Irwin Hospital and All India Institute of Medical Sciences (AIIMS) at Ansari Nagar. The latter of these was brand-new, having only been officially opened three years earlier. The former of these, Maulana Azad, was affiliated with University of Delhi and run by the government of Delhi. Admission was based on your examination results, but there were some additional points added (or subtracted) for how well you did in the interview portion of the application.

I have already established that I didn't love being put on the spot in this kind of public forum. In addition, many of the questions they asked were not even about medicine! We later found out that this was a way in which they could justify some backdoor admissions. In other words, if a politician wanted to arrange entrance for one of their supporter's children into medical school as a political favor, this would enable them to go about it. They could not falsify the test results; those were what they were. But they could affect the overall selection process by introducing the highly subjective element of an interview to accomplish their nefarious aims. For example, I was asked about my hobbies. When I said photography, they asked me, "Portrait or landscape?" They also asked me what the population of Delhi was. These questions had nothing whatsoever to do with medicine!

When the results came in, I was not selected. We saw that one student who had tested in the Second Class was actually admitted ahead of me. When my father was informed of this, he became livid. He wrote a letter to the local newspaper and met with the higher authorities. In order not to make this issue any bigger than it already was, the authorities reduced the points given to the interview process. I was then advanced and selected. We paid the admission fee at AIIMS and canceled my application to Maulana Azad Medical College.

I learned a lot about life from my father during these events. For one thing, his emphasis on principles was admirable. Being a lawyer, he believed that processes should not be able to be bent by those with ulterior motives. I also admired his persistence and how he demonstrated his belief that you should never give up on something if you feel in your conscious mind that you are right. Many people probably harbor principles and would like to be persistent, but when it actually comes down to it, they yield to a situation. Not my father. He felt an injustice had been done, and he would not stop until he exposed it.

Another lesson I learned about life from this experience was to always keep a second option open in case the first option proves unavailable. This strategy would come to my rescue many times over the years, especially in the competitive field of medicine. In this case of my education, while things were proceeding with my application to Maulana Azad Medical College, I was admitted to my second option of AIIMS. As an added benefit, my sister Ramesh was already there!

So that was where I ended up going. Because I already had a big sister at the school, I was spared the hazing—or what was called "ragging" in those days—that most newcomers had to go through. Our time at AIIMS became another formative experience for my sister and I to share together.

She, like I, had the desire to be the best in our chosen occupation. She finished her training, including her internship and a house job at the Institute, and then went on to do postgraduate work, obtaining a Master of Surgery. Further training took her to London, where she passed the Royal College of Surgeons of England examination as part of her Fellowship of the Royal Colleges of Surgeons qualification, then on to the famous Memorial Sloan Kettering Hospital in New York for an additional fellowship in surgical oncology. She then entered surgical oncology practice in Delhi, where she continues to practice. She was recently recognized for her outstanding contributions in teaching with a Lifetime Achievement Award from Apollo Hospitals Enterprise Limited in India.

All the while, she continues to be my guide and my best friend. Later in life we would have frank discussions about the family's illnesses and treatments. It is wonderful to have an informed confidante to communicate with about such personal matters. And to have that person be someone whose path I have followed for so many years is a true blessing.

Chapter Five

attended AIIMS for the next four years, from 1959 to 1963. As a public medical research university and hospital, AIIMS operated autonomously under the Ministry of Health and Family Welfare, but because it was a national institution, attendance policies were established by the government. Of fifty open slots per year, thirty-five were awarded to applicants based on the results of an examination. The remaining fifteen slots were reserved for either foreigners, such as those from Nepal, Sri Lanka, Malaysia, and Fiji, in order to enable an exchange program with institutions in those countries, or to citizens of a lower caste. Since India's lower castes had been systematically disadvantaged for so long, the state had created this special quota, a kind of affirmative action, mandated by the constitution.

Going to medical school was intense and all-consuming. I have often wondered if the pressure of medical school was what created the feeling of a kind of club among the students there. It started right at the beginning with the ragging tradition I mentioned previously. This was the routine greeting for newcomers by the senior class, meant as an introduction to the institute. It did sometimes get out of control, but I was spared the worst of it thanks to my sister and a few of her classmates, who would keep me in their rooms to protect me.

They couldn't keep me from all harm, however, and I'm not sure I would have wanted them to, as I might never have attained the full "initiation" if they had. During one ragging experience, I was told to come down to the grounds in front of Hostel No. 2. (My room was in Hostel No. 2, Room 32.) I thought I was going to meet all the seniors and wanted to introduce myself properly, so I pressed my pajama and kurta set with an iron. The seniors then asked me to go into the mud pond and wrestle with my classmates! My all-white clothes emerged completely dark.

Another time, the seniors had hired a barber to do all kinds of involuntary haircuts on the first-year students. When my turn came, they shaved off one half of my mustache. You may recall that I started wearing facial hair following the tradition established by my brother MK; by my first year at AIIMS, I had really gotten good at trimming it with special scissors. Well, with half of it gone after the ragging, I had to get the rest of my mustache shaved off completely. That would be the first and last time in my adult life I would go without one. And wouldn't you know it, that was the exact weekend I was going to visit MK after the birth of his son Prag. It was an odd experience, to say the least, to surprise my family with a clean face!

Once the whole ragging process settled down, those very same seniors who had been our tormentors would become our lifelong friends. They were now eager to help in any way they could. I would see them when we played table tennis, shuttlecock (another name for badminton), cricket, carrom board, or when we lifted weights.

There were three required professional tracks over the course of four and a half years. The first professional track consisted of anatomy, physiology, and biochemistry. I was first in biochemistry and second overall in the first professional examination. The second professional track consisted of pathology, pharmacology, microbiology, preventive and social medicine, and forensic medicine. I was fourth overall in standing in the second professional examination. The third professional track included medicine, surgery, obstetrics and gynecology, pediatrics, ophthalmology and otolaryngology. I was third in my class in the overall standing. My one-year course in premedical studies could not have prepared me for all these subjects, of course, but it did begin to solidify my study habits.

From the beginning, I knew that I did not have a photographic memory. Some of my classmates were able to devote far less time than I and still be able to absorb the material completely. In some courses, I needed to put in twice as many hours studying as some of my friends. But that was what it took, and there was no changing it. If I had to read a chapter three or four times to fully grasp the concepts, then that was what I was going to do.

On my first reading, I would scan and underline the pertinent information (except when I got to benefit from the parts my sister had already underlined in the books she handed down to me). In my second reading, I would review the underlined segments. In my third reading, I would take notes on the material in the margins of the book. Then, in my fourth reading, I would transfer the "headlines"—the key messages of the chapter—to index cards. That way, I would only have to study the cards before an exam. If a question did come to mind, I could reread that material in the book.

This may seem like a painstaking process, but I was not looking for the easy way out. I had fallen in love with medicine by this point, and I wanted to become the very best doctor I could be. My favorite subject of all was anatomy. I enjoyed every part of it. Some people enjoy the tastes of the food they eat; I wanted to know exactly where that food goes after we eat it. How is it broken down in the body? Which parts are converted into energy? What is excreted and how? The human body was a marvel to me.

Anatomy also helped me understand a lot about the disease process. If there was cancer in one part of the body, I wanted to know how far it could spread. Similarly, if a body was injured, how would the rest of the organism seek to compensate for the lack of mobility or function? My love of anatomy seemed to translate fairly effortlessly into my first experiences with a surgeon's knife. My classmate, Dr. Bhavnesh D. Chopra, who was my anatomy partner in those days, recently reminded me that I had always performed very clean dissections. Neither he nor

I knew in those days that I was destined to become a surgeon, but looking back now, it is apparent where some of the first signs of my future profession revealed themselves.

Although medical school was grueling, I still managed to make some friends to share my burdens with. We all had different study habits; my best time for thinking was from nine o'clock in the evening to midnight or later. My brain could still be actively functioning and processing information at two thirty in the morning! That usually meant I needed a short nap in the afternoon.

I spent a lot of time studying with my peers, such as Satish Kalhan and Om Prakash Talwar. One colleague, Udho Thadani, actually believed that the higher you went, the more knowledge would be absorbed into your brain. This was why you could often find him studying perched atop the *almirah* (a kind of wardrobe or chiffarobe). As an added advantage, he was usually left alone, because when someone entered the room looking for him, they did not think to look up that high; not seeing anyone, they would leave again! He also used to study with the radio blasting at full volume. The variations of methods we used to get us through those demanding and tedious hours of study were nearly endless.

We did other things to break up the monotony as well. For example, some of my classmates established a separate mess hall designed to mimic menus from the United States. They hired people to cook for them what they called "pseudo-American" food. At that time, America was thought of as a golden, faraway land of opportunity. I never ate in this cafeteria nor considered that a move to America would be in my future. Clearly, however, the threads of my future were beginning to weave themselves together, because that was exactly what happened.

There were a wide variety of activities designed to get our minds off studying for a little while, and my favorite was tennis. The tennis court could fill up fast in the evenings. My last class of the day was on surgical instruments, so I would attend in my tennis whites and take my racquet to class, then run to the courts as soon as the session let out to see if any were free. The year it was my turn to be captain of the tennis team, we won the intercollegiate championships! It was almost enough to forget that tomorrow there would be much more to learn. And the day after that, and the day after that . . .

Sometimes, no matter how hard we studied, though, we needed a little luck to help us get by. In this case, I am not talking about the unseen hand of destiny that I call Providence. I am just talking about having a fortunate moment, such as befell me one time in biochemistry. I had done my usual four-part study pattern and was confident I could remember most of the material. I did well in written examinations, but then came time for the oral examination. You probably know by now that this was not my favorite way to be tested; I could get tongue-tied in those moments.

Well, this time I had a surprise in store for me! During my studying, one particular factoid kept coming into my head: "indole and skatole." These are two kinds of bacterial species, organic compounds that cause fecal odor. I thought they were kind of a cute combination. Skatole has a distinct chemical structure (3 methyl-1H-indole), but it is part of a broader indole family.

Anyway, when my turn came for the oral examination, the examiners said to me: "We are tired. If you can answer just *one* question, we will give you the highest mark."

Guess what question they asked me? "What compound causes fecal odor?"

This had been the question in my head all day long! Not only did I get the highest marks in biochemistry but my name was also placed on the recognition board in the department. I guess you could say that all my studying paid off, although in a way that I could never have predicted.

Chapter Six

After I graduated from medical school, I had to complete a one-year rotating internship. This is required to qualify for bachelor of medicine and bachelor of surgery (MBBS), comparable to the MD degree in the U.S. Ostensibly, you begin these twelve one-month rotations without knowing what your eventual specialty will be, although I already had some inclination to go into cardiac surgery. My experience in this internship only confirmed that inclination, but it was also great to gain experience in related fields like anesthesia, where I learned the placement of arterial lines and intubations.

What I became convinced of early on in my medical career was that I didn't just want to talk about a patient's problems. I have earned high marks throughout my career for my "bedside manner" and the care I give to the individuals I treat. That is not what I mean when I say I didn't want to talk; what I mean is I didn't want to *just* talk. I wanted to be able to talk and then to act, in such a way that would ensure the patient got better.

If, for example, a patient presented with an acute gallbladder infection, there was a difference between a long discussion of a differential diagnosis or taking the gallbladder out, after which the patient returns to normal. With some specialties, I witnessed a different kind of paralysis on the part of the doctor. In oncology, for example, there weren't nearly as many chemotherapy agents then as there are now. That meant that a doctor would give a patient his or her diagnosis and prognosticate they had six or nine months to live. Sure enough, the patient would die in that time.

Surgery, on the other hand, was inspiring: You could know exactly what the problem was and what to do about it. I remember one early morning in my pediatric cardiac rotation, seeing a toddler who had turned blue from a congenital heart defect. The poor child could not breathe lying in his bed, yet by the very same afternoon, after an operation, the same child was running around with pink fingers. That was the kind of relief I was looking for and the difference I wanted to make.

One experience during my internship stayed with me perhaps more than any other and further directed my mind toward my future in cardiac surgery. Dr. Christian Barnard, an expert from South Africa, was visiting us to perform a rheumatic mitral valve surgery. Dr. N. Gopinath, the chief of cardiac surgery, allowed me to watch the procedure. In general, there was a lot of excitement about this event; many people had crowded into the operating room, some of whom were to help with the heart-lung machine. This machine consists of a pump and an oxygenator, which functions as the heart and replaces the function of the lungs during a cardiopulmonary bypass. The heart-lung machine thus allows the surgeon to stop the heart carefully while still maintaining the circulation of blood.

One individual, probably from the anesthesia department or maybe from cardiac surgery, saw two plastic tubes lying unconnected. He connected the two.

When Dr. Barnard was ready to operate, he issued the directive to "go on bypass."

There was silence in the room. The patient's heart started to shrink, and no blood was coming back to the body.

"Fill up the heart," Dr. Barnard insisted more than once.

"I am doing the best I can," was the answer from the perfusionist, the technician in charge of the heart-lung machine.

"Shut off the machine and fill up the heart! I can't operate like this," Dr. Barnard commanded. The procedure was aborted, and the patient was resuscitated for surgery at a later date. It turns out the operating room tech had mistakenly connected the tube on the floor to the suction machine instead of the venous return to the pump! The precise nature of this procedure, the setup of the heart-lung machine, and the quick decisions that had to be made to save the patient further steered my mind toward cardiac surgery. There has since been a marked improvement in the heart-lung machine. As for Dr. Barnard? He went on to great fame for performing the first cardiac transplant!

Once our final MBBS examinations were over, I saw some of my friends were preparing for a special test. When I inquired further, they told me it was the Educational Council for Foreign Medical Graduate examination being given at Vigyan Bhawan, a premier conference center of the Government of India in New Delhi. The purpose was to qualify for an applicant to go to the U.S. for further studies. While it was too late for me to do much studying, I signed up to take the exam anyway, and on March 25, 1964, I passed!

I still wasn't sure that I was going to America just yet. I knew that in any case I would need to take what is called a "house job." This one-year position is required to get your medical license in India, both in order to practice and to proceed with further postgraduate education. Because of my interest in cardiac surgery, I elected to take a job for six months in general surgery under Dr. Atm Prakash and six months in cardiology under Dr. Sujoy B. Roy, who had become famous for his work in High Altitude Pulmonary Edema.

Dr. Prakash was an excellent surgeon and a great teacher. His registrar wanted to build his own census, which recorded the cases he could claim he worked on—a crucial factor for later employment and promotion. Because of this situation, I was never allowed to do any independent surgery except for an occasional appendectomy or cholecystectomy. The hierarchy of the department was such that only the registrar and postgraduate students were allowed to help the professor. As a "house surgeon" (another way of describing my house job), I was at the mercy of the registrar.

I knew that just watching the surgery from a stool in the operating room was not going to make me a surgeon. I learned to take control of my own mind, however. In other words, I never complained in public but took advantage of whatever the situation had to offer. I already had the book knowledge, so when I watched a procedure, I focused instead on how the surgeon organized his instruments and the way his hands moved. I listened to the explanation of what he was doing, and if issues developed, such as massive bleeding, I watched how the surgeon handled the complication. In this way, I crafted the situation into something that would be beneficial to me in the long run.

I can remember one case that presented a challenge to me. The head of the department was treating a woman with acute necrotizing toxic ulcerative colitis; she required major colon surgery. He told the staff, "Take good care of her because she comes from the same village my family is from." Now, as surgeons, we are not supposed to have certain feelings for a patient. I always treated everyone the same—which came in handy later in my career when I had some very high-profile cases. We are to go through the same preparation, the same routine, no matter what. We concentrate on the anatomy and how the procedure is supposed to go, and that is that.

Well, in this case, the operation went well, but the patient developed septic shock nonetheless. All night, her blood pressure continued to drop. My instructions were to "keep her blood pressure up whatever it takes," and to keep a record of the pulse and blood pressure. Before the professor came around for his morning rounds, her blood pressure was still quite low, even though I had boosted the Levophed drip (a vasoconstrictor used to treat life-threatening low blood pressure, also known as hypotension). I was then instructed by a junior staff member to rewrite all the vital signs "to make the chart look good" for the upcoming rounds. I did so, and I have regretted it all these years. That was not who I was, and it took only one time to learn that lesson.

The final service rotation at my house job was with Dr. Sujoy B. Roy, and his tutelage was excellent. I learned a lot about the terms of cardiology, the physical examination of heart murmurs, the Swan-Ganz catheter for cardiac output monitoring, and various catheterization techniques. I remember coming to the ward early in the morning, reviewing the charts and laboratory reports in a summary form for the professor, and generally having a smooth and profitable experience during our rounds. The learning and interpretation of the electrocardiogram was an extra benefit.

Unfortunately, Professor Roy developed jaundice and had to be treated at home. My colleague, Dr. Panangipalli Venugopal, and I were supposed to draw the blood samples at Professor Roy's house, take them to the laboratory by hand and then go back to the laboratory to get the report by the evening. He was still being treated when our posting at the department was over. Overall, it was a good learning experience for a future cardiac surgeon!

■　　■　　■

Chapter Seven

believe it is always crucial to have two options in life. You can call them Plan A and Plan B, but I would say Plan A is not complete without also having Plan B in place. That is the only way to truly be prepared because there is only so much you can do to change a situation. Sometimes, you will have to take what life gives you. For example, after completing my house job, I still did not have enough surgery cases under my belt. I thought that if I went to England or to the U.S. I could gather many more cases to my name. But what if that option did not materialize? Then I would need another route by which to pursue my path in medicine.

Around the same time, I learned of a newly created post-graduate medical center, the Post Graduate Institute (PGI), later known as the Post Graduate Institute of Medical Education and Research (PGIMER). It had been created through the efforts of the Chief Minister of Punjab, Sardar Partap Singh Kairon. This became another autonomous body (similar to AIIMS) under an act of parliament and was under the control of the Government of India's Ministry of Health and Family Welfare. It had only been in existence since 1962, less than five years, but it had already developed a great reputation. Once again, I had two options: I could spend two more years completing my master of science (MS) at PGI or three years at AIIMS in Delhi. I selected PGI in Chandigarh, a city about 250 kilometers north of Delhi. As luck would have it, my elder brother Manohar Lal had his posting in Chandigarh at the same time, which was a great advantage. He had a motorbike that I was allowed to drive, and I used to go to his house over the weekends to rest and recuperate.

During the MS course, you were allowed to select a subspecialty and a research topic. I selected cardiothoracic surgery and wrote my thesis entitled "Evaluation of Various Types of Grafts in the Reconstruction of Cervical Esophagus in Dogs." My work was supervised by Dr. Santokh Singh Anand, the Director of Surgery, and by Drs. I. A. Chitamber and R. N. Chakrabarti.

Our experiments were performed on dogs, which were easily available from the street in India. We went along with the dog catcher to round up these animals. That we would then subject them to scientific experimentation was not so out of the ordinary. It was—and still is—very common to do a new surgical procedure on an animal first. Certainly, nobody would have questioned you in the late 1960s in India; this was the normal routine.

In my experiment, thirty-three dogs were divided into four groups and one control group. All dogs survived the procedure in the controlled group and were electively sacrificed in 20–58 days. In the Dacron graft group, one died. The postmortem revealed moderate stenosis, which could be dilated. All survived in the Aortic Heterograft (from another dog) group and developed severe stenosis at 25 and 39 days. In the Fascia Lata group (with metallic stent), one died and the remaining five survived, lasting 5 to 12 days (one escaped). In the free large bowel graft, no dog survived because of venous thrombosis and bowel necrosis due to the technical challenges of arterial and venous anastomosis.

These experiments were done under very basic conditions in a laboratory setting, which allowed me to gain a lot of useful experience. They helped me hone my craft, just as working on cadavers would have been helpful in another circumstance. The assistance from my classmate at this time, Dr. Venugopal, was invaluable. Together we learned the anatomy of the esophagus and its precarious vascular blood supply, bowel anastomosis procedures, microvascular suturing techniques, and how to make different materials for the grafts ourselves.

Our work was presented at one of the Patiala Cardiothoracic and Esophageal meetings. Unfortunately, it did not proceed to publication because of the relatively small number of animals we had in our experiment. It was, however, the first time I was involved with the long-term follow-up of subjects. All in all, it was a very fruitful endeavor that would later contribute to my skill set, and to my being able to save human lives.

While I was at PGI, two events of particular note stand out to me. The first came when I was driving my brother's motorbike. Dr. Venugopal was my passenger. It was just a normal day for us—we were going to the mall. In India, we drive on the left-hand side of the road. I will see if I can describe what happened to you: There was a large bus in front of me. The bus was slowing down, and I presumed it was giving me the signal to pass, which meant I would have sped up and passed on its right side. But actually, it was swinging wide to go right. By the time I realized this, it was too late. Our motorbike hit the bus, and both Dr. Venugopal and I were thrown in the air. The motorbike actually continued to skid all the way under the bus, although it—like us—emerged from the accident unharmed. It truly was a miracle; I believe Providence intervened in this situation. If not for the sake of keeping me in one piece, then at least to preserve the health of Dr. Venugopal, who went on to become a famous cardiac surgeon who performed the first heart transplant in India!

The second incident I remember was just before our final examinations, when I developed intense tooth pain. My normal routine of taking a short catnap in the afternoon and studying late into the night was disturbed. That was my preferred method to absorb a lot of information, but now I was thrown off. One might even say I was having a meltdown. With such pain, I could neither sleep nor study, and I was afraid I would forget everything.

Somehow, my mother found out about my situation, perhaps from a neighbor of ours who knew my family. She and my sister Satish immediately took a public bus from Delhi, which in those days took nearly a full day to reach where I was studying in the north of the country. (Even today it takes over five hours, and the roads were not nearly as refined then as they are now.)

The first thing my mother told me was not to study any more, especially the night before an exam. She advised that I should go see a movie, or do whatever I wanted, provided it was an activity to take my mind off the pressure rather than increase it. She knew I had already studied the material in my books four times over; this was my process, as I described earlier. With the situation a little becalmed, we were able to find a resident in dentistry to extract the offending tooth. Then, with the help of pain medications, I was able to sleep. My mother and sister continued to stay with me, consoling me and telling me that everything would be fine. And they were right! While the examinations were graded purely on a pass/fail basis, one internal examiner told me that I had the best score in my class.

There was only so much experience to be gained from cardiac and thoracic surgery books, however. Unfortunately, the operating-room experience at PGI was negligible, especially as it concerned open-heart surgery. I recall something the chief, Dr. Chitamber, said at the time that left an indelible impression on me. Dr. Chitamber had trained abroad and was a highly experienced, excellent technician, especially in surgical interventions on children. He told me: "You can do a great job in the operating room, but these children may still die because of the nonavailability of instant blood reports, especially blood gas reports." (I believe, at that time, the instant blood gas machine was not available in the operating room.)

This solidified my realization that it was time to go to the U.S. I could not bear to witness children dying in post-op simply because we lacked the necessary machinery or administration. In America, I felt sure that I would have the support to keep these kids healthy. England was another option, although at that time—and possibly still today—Indian nationals experienced a fair amount of discrimination. It could have been due to the legacy of the British Empire, but whatever the reason, we were not considered as equals. Americans, on the other hand, had less exposure to Indians, and therefore I believed there would be less immediate prejudice. In addition, at this time (1968–1970), I believe there was a shortage of physicians in the U.S. They were actually inviting foreigners to come to their country to fill all of their openings. Another advantage the U.S. had over England was that the British have a national health service; in practical terms, that meant you could never become an attending physician unless you were born in England. You might rise as high as a registrar, but that would be about it. That contrasted with the U.S. where, if you were good, you could go any place you wanted.

I started searching for places to apply for a surgical residency in the U.S. and ended up applying to several institutions. I knew if the reply envelope was thin, it would be an automatic rejection. A thick envelope was an excellent sign because it might contain application forms that needed to be completed. The thin envelopes were many, but as always, I had a Plan B. I decided that, to gain much-needed experience operating on patients—and to qualify to operate independently—I would pursue a postgraduate masters in cardiovascular and thoracic surgery (MCh, or Master of Chirugiae) at AIIMS. All the while, I networked with anyone who seemed willing to assist me, whether they were friends who had already left India for the U.S., or so-called Pool Officers, surgeons who had done their training abroad and come back to India looking for full-time government positions. I would take all the help I could get!

Chapter Eight

After finishing my postgraduate studies, I returned home to Delhi. I had no job, and I had not yet received a positive response from abroad. Even when I had no immediate prospects, however, I always had my network. That is something I often advise others about as well: When you allow people to help you, your odds of finding something—and, eventually, the right thing—increase exponentially. It is up to you to make and keep these connections. Then, when opportunities become available, they'll think of you!

In my case, one of my brothers had a friend who was the chief of neurosurgery at the Govind Ballabh Pant Hospital in Delhi. He said I could work with him while I looked for a job in cardiac surgery, and so I was able to get a temporary appointment as a registrar in neurosurgery until something became available in cardiac surgery under Professor Joginder Bhayana. Even when that happened, though, the position was still only a fellowship and not a residency.

During this time, my father suggested a clinic for me in Delhi. I had not told him or my mother about my desire to go to America yet. In fact, I actively kept this idea secret from my parents because I knew they preferred I stay in India. It is a feature of our culture that when the parents get older, and the children have become settled, the offspring will in turn take care of their elders. If I was not in the country, I wouldn't be able to help them. As it turned out, my brother HK would become the person who would devote himself to preserve our parents in their old age.

For these reasons, I kept my correspondence address at the PGI hostel so that no one would know of my plans. I wanted all the details to be set—to have my travel organized and my room and board established—before I broached the subject to my family. Parents can usually exert control when they are giving you money. If I was able to arrange everything ahead of time, they wouldn't be able to fall back on the excuse that they didn't have enough money.

As I mentioned before, a lot of opportunities in life come from who you know. In all fields—and the medical field is no exception—when someone is looking to fill an opening, they ask those immediately around them. It just so happened that one of my classmates from medical school, Dr. Manjit Singh Bains, had left India for the U.S. two years earlier. He was now working at Rochester General Hospital, in Rochester, New York. Dr. Bains had built a reputation as an excellent surgeon, providing quality care to his patients, and he had the respect and trust of the chief of surgery, Dr. Raymond Hinshaw.

One day, he told the chief, "If you are looking for a resident, I know of one who is very good."

And he was! Without any further interview, my application was accepted. Since I had three years of extra training, including my masters in surgery, I was spared having to go through an internship. Instead, I went straight to my first year of residency in general surgery.

Since I had not told my family yet, I requested and obtained a one-way fare from the hospital. They would also provide a one-bedroom apartment for me to stay in near the facility, a cleaning service, and free meals at the hospital, along with a nominal stipend. Once everything was set, then—and only then—did I tell my mother and father that I was going abroad. They were shocked, but they quickly came around to the idea, especially as I presented my reasoning. "I have degrees," I told them, "but I do not yet have operating-room experience. This will give me all the experience I could possibly need."

It really felt like a miracle that the first Chawla family member, who had never traveled abroad or even ridden in an airplane, was about to go to the U.S. with airline tickets provided by a hospital. I possessed the eight dollars allowed in foreign exchange at the time and an extra twenty dollars from the booking agent—and that was it!

There was great fanfare at the airport while my family members and classmates gathered to say goodbye. I had informed my friend and study partner, Dr. Satish Kalhan, who was getting his training in England, that I would have a layover of a couple of days in London, and perhaps I could meet him at the airport.

Not so quick! Our plane developed engine trouble and had to land in Pakistan. The captain announced that the delay would only last a few hours when, in fact, it lasted twelve. We were escorted to a hotel that the airline paid for. There were still great hostilities between Pakistan and India in those days, and because neither side trusted each other, the Pakistani government took our passports away. That way, in case we were terrorists or spies, we wouldn't try to leave the hotel and infiltrate the countryside.

There was no way I could communicate with my friend Dr. Kalhan because there were no cell phones nor any email in those days.

Amazingly, Dr. Kalhan was kind enough to hang around for all that time—twelve hours at the airport in London! He greeted me when I got off the plane. I spent two nights there, the first with our classmate Dr. Dhirendra Bana. The following day, Dr. Kalhan took me shopping and bought me a warm jacket—for he knew what I did not, that my final destination in Rochester, New York, gets very cold in winter. He also purchased a few wrinkle-free shirts for me, since I would be living alone in my apartment and washing my own clothes.

The kindness shown to me throughout those days was profoundly touching. It is something I have never forgotten, and something that I have pledged to pay forward to those individuals just getting started on their way. In fact, coming to Rochester was the greatest gift I received as a new physician.

I was able to meet new people and learn a new culture. There was a new program in the neighborhood where local families would welcome foreign physicians to their houses, take us shopping—as we did not have a car—and invite us to social occasions at their houses.

Two families in particular come to mind: the Rossis, who had a son and daughter, and the Callans, who had two sons and one daughter. Not only did they invite me to functions, but George Callan even took me to buy my first car, as that was his area of employment. Now, what kind of car you own is very important in the culture I was coming from. Your future father-in-law would usually look at externals to see how his prospective new son-in-law was doing, and in this case, he would want to see a new Chevy Impala. It could be something comparable, but the Impala is the car people saw in all the movies in India. So I saved my stipend religiously, and that is what I purchased for two thousand dollars. I do not remember the color; I just remember that it could not be black or red in order to fit the ideal mold of a son-in-law!

Dr. Bains kept close tabs on me for the next two years and continued to help me settle in. There were a few other Indian physicians at the hospital as well, some single, some married. One day, one of them—my senior resident, Shashi Kumar—and his wife took me to a barbecue at one of their friends' houses. The house had an outdoor swimming pool that was at least six feet deep. I had never been in any body of water, let alone tried to swim. I should also note that, although I didn't drink at the time, there was beer there in abundance.

Someone suggested, "Hey, let's all go in the swimming pool!"

I mentioned that I didn't know how to swim. To which they replied, "Don't worry! The pool is not that deep . . . just hold on to the side railing."

It was getting dark now. The drinking was in full swing. I remember distinctly that they started playing a game of water polo. I tried to stay very close to the wall, as I had been instructed, and hold on to the railing, but my hands slipped, and I went under the water.

I was in a panic! In Delhi, there are no oceans. In the hot season, you might jump in and out of a pond, but there is hardly any water level there to speak of. There is certainly not enough cause to give kids swimming lessons. Under the surface of the pool, I tried to shout, but nobody could hear me. Perhaps they thought I was just playing a game or had dived down to get the ball. All I know is, they would have found my body floating in the morning if I hadn't felt some uprush from underneath me, like a guardian angel lifting me, until I rose to the surface again and was helped out of the pool. I still do not know what force was watching over me that day. But I do know that I cannot think of that episode without immediately suffocating. I have considered taking swimming lessons since then, but each time that automatic reaction seizes me, and I can't do it. I have resigned myself to being aquaphobic.

My father, Darya Datta Chawla, in New Delhi; 1960s

My mother, Parbati Devi, New Delhi; 1960s

My paternal grandmother in New Delhi; circa 1950

Me with my sisters, Ramesh and Satish, and our brother Manohar, New Delhi; circa 1952

My class picture from the Dayanand Anglo Vedic (DAV) Higher Secondary School; circa 1952

Pre-med class photo from Hans Raj College, Delhi; 1958

Student names from Hans Raj College

My admission picture at the All India Institute of Medical
Sciences, New Delhi; 1960

Admissions class at the All India Institute of Medical Sciences, New Delhi; 1959

All six siblings together: Me (in the center), our father, Satish, Hari Kishan, Maharaj Kishan, Manohar Lal, and Ramesh

Chapter Nine

The surgical experience was exceptional at Rochester General Hospital. All of the attending physicians were experienced, great surgeons. A few that come to mind are Drs. Farlow, Africano, Sahler, Bodon, and Subtelny. To a man, they were all eager to help the residents. I was even able to operate as the first surgeon on many patients, gaining the invaluable experience I had sought for many years.

Such a supervised operation might look like this: One patient of Dr. Farlow's had a small bowel obstruction requiring a resection, which means the removal of tissue or all or part of an organ. While we were scrubbing our hands prior to surgery, Dr. Farlow asked me, "Do you know everything about this patient's history?"

"Yes, sir," I replied. I was never going to have a lack of preparation be the reason why I couldn't be granted an opportunity that might come my way.

"Have you done a bowel resection before?"

"No, sir," I replied. I have always believed that honesty is the best policy, even more so when an individual's health is at stake.

To my surprise, however, Dr. Farlow said, "Well, why don't you start, and we'll see how far we can go."

The procedure must have gone very well because when I had finished, Dr. Farlow said, "You are lying. You must have done this operation before."

I responded, "Sir, I have a lot of theoretical knowledge. And I have seen many surgeons perform these operations. But I have not personally been the primary surgeon." From then on, I did most of Dr. Farlow's cases.

My confidence grew with every procedure I did. I received praise for being naturally gifted—although I amplified that with strenuous study, so I can't say with certainty which abilities I came into this life with versus which were developed through painstaking effort. Because of my religious background, I hold fast to the idea of reincarnation; it may very well be that I was a physician in a previous life. Nonetheless, each new lifetime allows us the opportunity to either wake up a previous skill or allow it to remain dormant. I was determined to do the former.

A concrete example was when Dr. Weiner gave me the opportunity to implant a pacemaker. This procedure involves inserting a wire into the blood vessel and advancing it to attach to the heart. Now, you were not supposed to advance the wire until you looked at its positioning under a fluoroscope (a fluorescent screen for viewing images similar to an X-ray but without capturing images). But I did not know that. So when the doctor said, "OK, Surendra, start the procedure," I simply maneuvered the catheter inside its plastic tube with my naked eye.

"Stop!" I was told. "You need to watch your progress under the X-ray or you could perforate the ventricle!"

When I did so, however, I found that I had already slid the lead wire into perfect position. I had seen it done so many times, and I had the spatial relations to be able to determine how far the wire should go. Of course, I always used the fluoroscope after that, both to follow the hospital's protocols and to be extra sure I was doing the best job I could. But at the same time, I did seem to naturally know what I was doing in the surgery theater.

During our training in Rochester General Hospital, we were obliged to rotate through the Memorial Sloan Kettering Cancer Center for six months. I worked there from January to June of 1970. It was a wonderfully compact training in various departments, such as Head and Neck under Dr. Elliot Strong; Gastric and Mixed Tumor under Dr. Joe Fortner; Breast Surgery under Drs. Guy Robbins and Roy Ashikari; Bone and Joint under Dr. Ted Miller; Colorectal under Dr. Maus Stearns; and Thoracic Surgery under Dr. Edward Beattie.

Regarding this last individual, I was only with Dr. Beattie for my one-month rotation, the same as the others. But I remember being thoroughly impressed by how well he knew all the statistics and data from all the services. I also found it very encouraging the way he gave credit to whoever had collected the data or done the research in question. Perhaps this combination of genius and humility is why he was not only the chief of thoracic surgery but also the surgeon in charge of the whole institution! I asked for a letter of reference from every doctor whose area I rotated through—to get ahead of the story a little, Dr. Beattie's letter would prove particularly valuable.

At Sloan Kettering, I distinctly remember the weekend classes, which featured excellent slides for every topic. They were each worth taking pictures of. There was no way to get the lecture slides from the professor in those days, so I entrusted my photography skills to capture these images. Having a visual reference on hand made for such a concrete way to remember the various pathologies.

Some of my contemporaries stayed at Sloan Kettering and became known in their own right. Dr. Bains remained with the Department of Thoracic Surgery and became the inventor of new procedures, a real doctor's doctor who routinely saved other surgeons when they were in trouble in the operating room. Dr. Jatin Shah, another contemporary of mine, eventually became chief of head and neck surgery at Sloan Kettering, publishing books in the field for both residents and students.

I returned to the University of Rochester and requested a posting with Dr. Charles Robb, the chief of surgery there, so I could concentrate for a few months in cardiac and vascular surgery. Dr. Robb's specialty at the time was vascular surgery, especially carotid endarterectomies, and he was both an excellent teacher and a "clean" surgeon.

I remember two more episodes that occurred during my time at Rochester that continued to expand my perspective and experience through the graciousness of my mentors there.

The first was a particular cardiac surgery attended by Dr. Larry Zaroff. We were performing a closure of the patent foramen ovale, or PFO. There is a hole between the left and right atria (the upper chambers) of the heart that exists in everyone in utero, but it almost always closes shortly after birth. PFO is what the hole is called when it fails to close naturally. Dr. Zaroff set up all the connections for the heart-lung machine and opened the right atrium. Then he said to me: "Now close that hole!"

That was my first experience with open heart surgery.

I also had my first experience performing a takedown of the internal mammary artery prior to a coronary bypass grafting, which, in 1972, was the latest method of surgical procedure for coronary revascularization. This came under the watchful guidance of Dr. Amarendra Sengupta, who was one of the few cardiac surgeons trained at the Cleveland Clinic. The trust that these men showed me could truly never be repaid.

In the midst of all this hands-on learning, I was also maturing in a different way. I was ready to find a potential life partner. I wanted to be with someone educated but also brave—my future plans were uncertain in those days. About the only thing that was certain was that I would have to work many hours as a cardiac surgeon. I thought if I could find someone who understood those considerations, then we could make the rest work.

Ours was not a formal arranged marriage, but my family had nonetheless indicated they had a few potential matches in mind who could be suitable for me. Anticipating I might find a bride, I bought one ticket from the U.S. to India and two return tickets. The second return ticket had no name on it, which is not only unheard of these days but also not allowed!

I first met Ranjana in India on December 30, 1970. She was accompanied to my family home by her mother, her younger sister, and an uncle who was a physician. They came from Allahabad, in Uttar Pradesh, to meet us at our house in Karol Bagh, a distance of more than 400 miles. These days, it takes a day to make that drive—in those days, it was an overnight journey.

Ranjana had been educated at a convent, which meant she spoke English well, and she had learned about America through books and films. In addition, she was attractive and had a masters in psychology. What more could I ask for?

I spoke with her about my future plans and the hard work that lay ahead if I got a residency in cardiac surgery. I was honest about the fact that I had not yet decided whether I would return to practice in India or stay in the U.S. Ranjana agreed to weather those storms with me as they came, and our family started the celebration.

Our marriage was proposed and solemnized all in the space of nine days, on January 8, 1971. I put my new wife's name on the second ticket, and we had our honeymoon in Italy and Switzerland. Following that, we continued on to the U.S. and the somewhat less romantic destination of Rochester in the wintertime.

At this time, I applied for the Fellowship of Royal Colleges of Surgeons (FRCS). This is the professional qualification required to practice as a surgeon in the United Kingdom and the Republic of Ireland. The Royal College recognized the postgraduate training of my Master of Surgery, as well as my two years of training in America. I then needed to pass both a written and an oral examination before I was awarded a special certificate in general surgery. (After several years the organization gave all the special certificate holders full certification.) After finishing my cardiac surgery residency, I applied and passed the examination of Fellow of Royal Colleges of Surgeons in the specialty of cardiothoracic surgery. I pursued this accreditation because, at the time, I did not yet know whether I would be staying in the United States for the next few years—let alone the balance of my career! All I knew then was that my time at Rochester was coming to a close. They gave me an offer to join a general surgical group, but I had my heart set on a residency in cardiothoracic surgery. And so, my search continued.

Chapter Ten

The time had come to apply for residencies in cardiothoracic surgery programs. My local attending physicians did not have the network to provide direct referrals, so I applied myself—both literally and figuratively—and sent in my credentials to at least eighty-five programs.

Obviously, in such a situation, almost all responses are rejections. I would not say that I had a thick skin that allowed me to withstand hearing "no" so often. Rather, I would say that everyone else I knew was going through the same thing at the same time. So I had company, and I knew not to take the rejections too personally. Another factor that helped to fuel my persistence was the fact that the practice of cardiothoracic surgery was limited at the time. It was limited in terms of what we could do, and it was limited in the number of people we could help. So, naturally, what followed was a limited number of residences available to meet this lesser demand. I would witness over the course of my professional career an explosion in all areas pertaining to my surgical field—but I won't get ahead of the story.

Out of my eighty-five applications, I received four acceptances, although all came with certain caveats. The University of Maryland, under Dr. Joseph S. McLaughlin, offered me a position of "Assistant Resident" in Thoracic Surgery for one year. "Assuming satisfactory performance," he wrote to me, "the senior year of residency is automatically offered." The word *assuming* was a concern to me. Did that mean they would make a subjective decision at the end of the first year? And who would be in charge of making that decision? What if I was not offered the second year—would finding another place elsewhere then be twice as difficult, since being released might reflect negatively on my curriculum vitae?

The second qualified acceptance came from the University of Mississippi Medical Center, under Dr. James Hardy. He wanted another resident position, but the Residency Review Committee had refused to add one more. So instead, Dr. Hardy had decided to start a fellowship program. He wrote to me that "the clinical experience would be the same, but the fellow would, of course, not be qualified to take the examination of the Board of Surgery at the end of the two-year fellowship." This was a no-brainer; it was getting harder and harder to get the kind of job I wanted unless I was board certified.

The Cleveland Clinic, under Dr. Floyd Loop, was my third acceptance. They, too, could only offer me a fellowship in the Department of Thoracic and Cardiovascular Surgery. There was a stipend of a not-insubstantial sum: $13,000 a year in those days, which would be nearly $100,000 today. But it was still only a fellowship and not a residency, so it wasn't a viable option.

The fourth acceptance came from the University of Alberta Hospital, under the direction of Dr. John Carter Callaghan. There I was at least offered the position of Senior Assistant Resident. In addition, they would help me with my Canadian visa. The problem was that this position was only being offered for one year. I might have trouble transferring the experience I gained there to another institution, but, having no other good option, it seemed better to spend the next year of my professional career in Canada.

I signed the contract with the University of Alberta, but my heart was not in it. Thus, I continued to pursue my preferred option, which was to stay in the U.S. I was still on the hunt for a good residency program in cardiothoracic surgery, so, on my own, I traveled around to various hospitals and surgeons. I made it a practice to simply let places know I was coming to see if they would be able to make any time to meet with me.

For example, I had applied with Dr. L. Penfield Faber, who was chairman of the House Staff Committee at Chicago's Presbyterian-St. Luke's Hospital in early 1971, but I was refused a position in his residency program. I wrote to him, saying, "I will be visiting Chicago for another occasion on September 27 and would like to visit your hospital for an interview."

He wrote back, "We regret that we were unable to place you in our cardiothoracic surgery program for the year beginning July

1972. I assume you would not wish to complete your interview scheduled for September 27. If you do wish to visit the hospital on that date, please let me know."

This I felt, at last, was a break! I wrote back, "I am sorry to learn that your residency program for the year 1972 has been filled up. I would still like to visit your hospital for the interview, however."

As soon as I arrived and sat down, I recall Dr. Faber mentioning, "We do not have a spot for you. There is no need for your interview."

I somehow insisted that I had come a long distance from Rochester to Chicago and asked if he could please have my file pulled out and write a note that I was here with his comments. With great hesitation, his secretary brought the file, he scribbled a few notes, and the meeting was finished.

At the time, I felt I had nothing to lose. Why couldn't I just go and visit? I had since gotten married, and we had decided to take a tour of the country. I am not sure I can explain why I wrote to a variety of people to ask if I could come in for an interview or go on a tour of their operating room. In my mind, I kept thinking, *Just pursue it. You never know what will come of it.*

I now know it was the voice of destiny speaking. It seemed clear that this door with Presbyterian-St. Luke's Hospital was closed. And yet, I soon received a letter from Dr. Hassan Najafi, the incoming chief of cardiothoracic and vascular service at Presbyterian-St. Luke's Hospital. He was looking for someone to work in his laboratory on calves to produce ischemia by occluding a single coronary artery to produce subendocardial myocardial infarction, and to find methods to prevent this condition. The position would be in Chicago for a period of one year. He was noncommittal as to whether this position may automatically lead to the residency program but promised he would look into it.

Persistence and Providence had joined hands. How else to explain the fact that Dr. Faber's note in my file had, in effect, moved it from the bottom of the pile to the top? How else to explain that Dr. Najafi had just taken the position of chief that year and needed someone for a laboratory position? And, even more incredibly, how else to explain that when Dr. Najafi started looking for his candidate from the recent applications for the residency program, he happened to notice a reference letter from Dr. Edward Beattie, the chief of surgery at the Sloan Kettering Memorial Hospital?

A few months after I started working with him, Dr. Najafi told me, "You know how I selected you? Dr. Beattie was my teacher and a mentor. Anyone referred by him is my resident."

What were the chances of repeating this good fortune?

I was left with two choices: I could go to the University of Alberta, where I had already signed a contract, or I could cancel the contract and take a chance in going to Chicago. I chose Chicago for a number of reasons, a primary one being that going there meant I would not have to leave the country. What's more, as an "independent surgeon," I would be allowed to perform surgery without assistance, which proved useful on many occasions during my practice. And lastly, I would be part of a research faculty—writing, publishing, and presenting papers.

Chapter Eleven

My year in Dr. Najafi's laboratory was a very fruitful one. I was able to complete research on my Masters of Surgery thesis topic, which involved the creation of subendocardial myocardial necrosis of the heart in calves by occluding the coronary artery while on cardiopulmonary bypass and then finding different ways to prevent this, whether through systemic cooling, profound local cooling, steroids, or a combination of these treatments. I had started this work at the University of Illinois, but it was cut short after the start of my residency in cardiothoracic surgery. I was also able to have a peer-reviewed paper published in the *Journal of Cardiovascular Surgery* with Dr. Najafi and Michael Haklin (who was my main assistant in the laboratory).

Besides this investigation, I took other projects upon myself as well, including inducing subendocardial myocardial infarction in hypertensive beagles, the hypertensive heart model being created by the Goldblatt method (removing one kidney and narrowing the second one). I also did experiments comparing knitted versus woven synthetic grafts, implanting them in the descending thoracic aorta. This was where we learned that the period of aortic cross clamping was critical for the prevention of paraplegia.

With all these experiments, I gained much valuable experience. I learned how to be an independent surgeon, for example, one who could function as my own anesthesiologist, assistant, and perfusionist. In effect, I was positioning myself to be a complete surgeon, which came in very handy later in my practice. Even though I would be surrounded by many talented helpers in the operating room, I knew it was good practice to ensure I could rely on myself during stressful periods that would require quick thinking.

Also, with all this technical repetition, I was able to get to know how to work with my hands better. This shortens the time of any procedure. There is always a balance as a surgeon between being methodical, not rushing, doing clean work, and at the same time getting it done in an expedient fashion. I never rushed any of my work for the hospital's sake or for any kind of glory. The case always had to be done perfectly, no matter what. I used to tell the residents that "no case is short, unless it finishes early." By the same token, less time on the operating table is better for the patients so they can get on with their healing journey.

Finally, somewhat paradoxically, all my independent work in the lab helped me become a better member of a surgical team.

The process in the operating room requires a kind of choreography in which different individuals are assigned different tasks. Having done them all, I now had a clearer idea of how everything worked together and so could better be the conductor in the operating theater.

As I mentioned, in my first experiences with medical school I always took a great liking to the subject of anatomy. Now, in spite of so many other projects, I also undertook the dissection of a human cadaver, dissembling the chest wall and thoracic cavity, including the heart, lungs, and the collection of nerve fibers known as the sympathetic chain, and the organs of the abdomen. I was even able to have this dissection videotaped by the audiovisual department of Rush Medical College in Chicago, Illinois. The recordings were used by students before later being donated to the University of Connecticut.

Most of my lab work was completed in the mornings; in the afternoon, the assistants in the main operating room were usually lacking. I received permission from the senior resident, Joe Amato, to be assigned as an assistant to any surgeon on many of these cases. The most memorable case was a young male, a drug addict, who had aortic valve endocarditis (an infection of the inner lining of the aortic valve in the heart) and required an aortic valve replacement.

Dr. Hushang Javid was the primary surgeon on the case. He said to me, "Dr. Chawla, why don't you start the case, and I will join you shortly."

Once he arrived, as a routine gesture, I started moving toward the side, where the assistant was supposed to stand.

He said, "No, stay," and then provided me with a series of commands: *open the chest . . . do not forget to give heparin (an anticoagulant) . . . go on bypass . . . gently cross clamp the aorta . . . open the aorta at this site . . . inspect the valve . . . excise the valve . . . remove the debris . . . put in the sutures . . . use the proper-size aortic homograft valve . . . lower the valve . . . tie the suture . . . close the aorta.*

Only when the procedure was over did I realize that I had done my first aortic valve replacement, before my residency had even started! Dr. Javid was one of many people who gave me opportunities to excel when they could see that I was ready. Not everyone showed up in my life as a willing mentor, of course. But those who did gave me a tremendous confidence boost. I tried to always bear this in mind when I was given the opportunity to mentor others later in life. Without risking any patient's health or well-being, I was able to help surgeons coming up behind me push themselves a little further than they thought they were ready to go and thus pass on the baton of superior medical care.

It was during this time in Chicago that our son, Sujit, was born. This was a fortunate period because my role did not involve any night calls, and I was able to spend meaningful time with him. I still have clear memories of coming home to feed him and being there to give him his very first haircut. In the evenings, Ranjana and I would dim the lights and sneak out of his room to let him sleep while we enjoyed dinner together.

While I had come to Chicago for a research position, my surgical technique clearly contributed to my positive reputation—which had now become known among the surgical staff attending physicians. Word spread that I would be a good candidate for their residency program. Toward the end of that year, 1973, Dr. Najafi called me in and told me they would give me the full residency in cardiothoracic and vascular surgery. The only catch was that instead of finishing in two years, my residency would finish in two-and-a-half years because they already had a candidate ahead of me who would finish in two years.

This was a gift and an offer I could not refuse. To be able to rotate through vascular surgery, thoracic surgery, cardiac surgery, and then through postings at the children's hospital was the opportunity I had been seeking for years. By the end, not only would I have enough vascular surgery cases to qualify for Vascular Surgery certification with the American Board of Surgery, but I would also be able to diversify and do abdominal aortic surgery and carotid endarterectomies.

And all of this would be under the guidance of Dr. Najafi, who had a wonderfully methodical approach that was apparent in his especially clean operations. In any meeting we ever had about surgical technique, he was there to give me advice. In addition to his superior methods, though, Dr. Najafi was a great researcher and an excellent teacher. He wrote a lot of papers, which is difficult to do when you already have a demanding caseload—even completing one paper a year can be a challenge because of the difficulty in producing the necessary data. Nonetheless, Dr. Najafi was just as comfortable in the lecture hall as he was in the operating room. He would go up on the podium before a packed audience and discuss his papers with a self-assured style that eluded me for most of my life. I watched with awe as he collected his information and organized it in such a way that it was instantly understandable, including all references to the previous literature on the topic.

He was so good at the public-facing aspects of the job that he eventually became one of the presidents of the Society of Thoracic Surgeons. One piece of advice he gave me that I have never forgotten applies to both writing and presenting. He said that there will be people who are going to be both agreeable and disagreeable to what you are trying to say, which is why you should be precise when you present your cases. And whether you are writing or presenting, don't goof around; grab the audience's interest right from the beginning and get them looking for more. If you are presenting, for example, the first slide should go off with a bang!

Chapter Twelve

My various rotations during my residency were memorable thanks to a few experiences in particular, as these experiences contributed to making me the doctor—and the man—I am today.

The six months I spent in vascular service were crucial to accumulating enough cases (fifty in major vascular surgery and sixty-three in minor vascular surgery) to qualify for obtaining privileges in private practice. The vascular boards requirement was just starting and I was grandfathered in, meaning I did not need to take an examination.

I spent a total of nine months in the Thoracic Services department at Presbyterian-St. Luke's Hospital, both before and after a rotation to Children's Hospital in Chicago. My attending physicians were Dr. Robert Jensik, Dr. L. Penfield Faber, and Dr. Frederick Kittle. Each one of these men made a distinct impact on me and were very well known in the medical community. In fact, someone once remarked that if you attended the weekly Saturday meetings at the hospital, you could never fail a future examination because all the attendings for the meeting were the examiners at the area hospitals, including the University of Illinois, Cook County Hospital, University of Chicago, Loyola University Medical Center, and Northwestern Memorial Hospital.

Dr. Jensik was a hard worker. He used to go to the nearby lung clinic where mostly burned-out pulmonary tuberculosis patients came. He would bring those patients to our hospital for bronchoscopy and excisions. It was interesting that he never did his own bronchoscopies, part of the preparatory work for the more serious surgeries. I think Dr. Jensik lacked the patience to do this relative grunt work, and he let his associate Dr. Faber do all of them for him.

Dr. Jensik's lack of patience, which was a virtue in terms of his exactitude, was directed at me one day. He was famous for a lung-sparing surgery known as pulmonary subsegmental segmentectomy. He would even perform this operation on cancer patients if it was indicated. As might be expected, many of these patients had lungs without clear-cut subsegments, meaning their lung resections (or removals) were difficult. On many occasions, there would be an air leak. I remember Dr. Jensik giving me a subsegmentectomy case to do, but partway through the operation, he commented with a stern voice, "Why are you not going through the fissures? You are causing so many more air leaks!" He guided me through the procedure, and I learned a very valuable lesson that day, even though it was not a very pleasant experience.

I remembered Dr. Faber instantly—he was the same surgeon who, as dean of admissions, had refused to interview me for the residency. I didn't blame him for his decision. On paper, the residencies were all filled up, and it looked like there were no openings. I still didn't know why I was so persistent, but in retrospect, I was glad I listened to the voice of Providence in my ear. In any regard, I did not hold Dr. Faber's earlier treatment of me against him. As it turned out, we got along very well. He was excellent in bronchoscopies, and I did a lot of work under his supervision. He was remarkably at ease when overseeing a junior surgeon during a case, and he was a good and patient teacher.

Dr. Frederick Kittle, who came from the University of Chicago, was very friendly as a resident surgeon. He took his time with both patients and residents alike during the ward round. Then, at the end of rounds, he would take the residents for lunch. That was another habit I carried along with me when I went into practice, providing meals for our physician assistants after a long case. I was learning from these great men both inside and outside of the operating room.

Once, Dr. Kittle asked me, "What is your first name?"

"Surendra," I replied.

He remarked that if I wanted to stay in this country, I should not have a lengthy name that no one could pronounce. He gave me my nickname, "Sandy," which some of my colleagues then started to call me. I never thought to take offense to this, as Dr.

Kittle was such a kindly person, and I had been raised to honor my teachers. So, Sandy it was!

My next rotation was in pediatric cardiac surgery. I found this branch of medicine fascinating. Our faculty was comprised of Dr. Farouk Idriss, who was the chief, and Dr. H. Nikaidoh, the assistant chief, along with senior resident Dr. Hamoudah and co-resident Dr. Susan Luck. It was a challenging field; babies are very tiny, and their resilience is almost nil if you make the wrong diagnosis. In addition, this was a very precise science. If, for example, the child has 100 cc (about 3.5 oz) too little fluid in the body, they are dehydrated, but if you give them 100 cc too much fluid, you'll put them into heart failure.

I had a strong desire to enter pediatric cardiac surgery, but as I mentioned previously, my senior resident talked me out of it, arguing that there would be so many fewer jobs available in that field, especially at the full-time university level. That shattered my enthusiasm, and I stayed the course for adult cardiac surgery.

The rotation in cardiac surgery came next. They had saved the best for last! This was the rotation I was waiting for. My attending physicians included many names I have related already, including Dr. Najafi and Dr. Javid. But there were others, such as Dr. William Dye, Dr. Milton Weinberg, Dr. Marshall D. Goldin, Dr. Cyrus Serry, and Dr. James A. Hunter.

I have already professed my admiration for Dr. Najafi, but I will add just one more thing he told me about why his operating field was the cleanest imaginable. "Dr. Chawla," he said, "while you are operating, imagine that some reporter or a photographer is watching the operative procedure. Do you think they want to see a clean field or a field full of spurting blood?" Someone once commented that when Dr. Najafi was operating it looked almost like he was operating on a cadaver, such was the absence of blood. I have followed in his footsteps and sought clean operations in my surgical practice ever since.

As to Dr. Javid, I would like to add that he designed his own shunt, a sterile device designed to serve as a temporary blood conduit during common carotid artery cross clamping. It was the first carotid shunt and still bears his name to this day: the Javid shunt. Before then, I never knew doctors could be inventors too! It put an idea in the back of my mind to develop a patent of my own—but we'll get to that later.

I remember Dr. Dye as easygoing. I never saw him angry. He trusted his residents to perform operations for him and was a good teacher.

Dr. Weinberg took a special liking to me and would let me do many of his cases. I remember once he said, "Why don't you do the bypass on this VIP patient (of some organization)?" This was during my senior years, what an honor!

Dr. Goldin was an energetic young surgeon, and sometimes that made him overconfident. Coronary bypass grafting was just coming into the arena of cardiac surgeons, and everyone was eager to learn and gain experience. I did single and sometimes double coronary bypass grafting with Dr. Goldin. That was where it stopped; for him, triple bypass was for the attendings only. (We rarely did quadruple bypass surgery in those days.)

Dr. Serry was the youngest of the attending physicians. To some degree, he represented the next wave of surgeons who had less fear and were ready to embrace the greater caseload that would soon be the fate of all cardiac surgeons. In fact, someone once asked him, "What is the indication for open-heart surgery?" (Meaning in what cases would it be safe to undertake such an operation.) To which Dr. Serry replied, "Any heart that has a heartbeat!" In his mind, no case was inoperable.

Finally, there was Dr. Hunter, who was not only a good surgeon but also an innovator like Dr. Javid. He was always planning new inventions. For example, he invented the Hunter-Sessions percutaneous vena cava occlusion device. This operated like a small balloon when inflated to prevent pulmonary embolism; it would stay in the inferior vena cava and deflate over a period of twelve months. I hope, even if you don't understand all of the science in this book, you can appreciate the thinkers I was surrounded by. They were not only surgeons; they were visionaries!

Chapter Thirteen

The end of my residency was fast approaching, and I did not have a job offer yet. Dr. Najafi knew that I had not secured employment, and he was kind enough to offer me an adjunct attending position for the next six months. His group, however, could not absorb me unless some other member left that year.

During the course of my job hunting, I sent letters of recommendation, including the one from Dr. Edward Beattie I had obtained while rotating through his Thoracic Services department at Memorial Sloan Kettering. I also attached a copy of all my procedures. This tally is akin to a CV or a resume; it showed my experience in very specific and unassailable terms:

SERVICE	SURGEON	ASSIST
Lungs, Mediastinum, Esophagus	60	31
Acquired heart Disease	188	125
Vascular Surgery	50	63
Pediatric Surgery		Mostly assisted

I had well-rounded experience and felt confident that I would meet some institution's criteria. The many cases I had worked on were sure to prove that I could function as an independent physician and would be a good fit for someone's practice. I sent letters to eighty-seven hospitals in twenty-three states and waited for their response.

The geographical swath I went out to could not have been broader: Alabama, California, Connecticut, Florida, Illinois, Indiana, Kansas, Kentucky, Louisiana, Maryland, Massachusetts, Michigan, Missouri, New Jersey, New York, North Carolina, South Carolina, Ohio, Pennsylvania, Tennessee Texas, Virginia, and Wisconsin. I was not looking for any particular region, climate, salary, vacation time, or partnership. All I sought was a well-known place where I could contribute my talents and passion for medicine.

My career journey was marked throughout by challenges—it almost made the medicine seem easy by comparison! It was a challenge to find the right school and then the right internship and then the right residency. To encounter a challenge finding the right job should not have surprised me. I felt sure that patient growth was occurring, meaning that the more available certain procedures became, the more people we could help—and that would ensure there would be more jobs in the future. I just had to be patient and persevere.

I also understood that many institutions wanted to give jobs to their own residents first, if in fact they had any openings at all. These individuals had proven themselves in a very quantifiable way to the immediate people making the hiring decisions. But I was still in for a shock when I only received four responses to the eighty-seven letters I had sent.

The first offer came from Harold Conn at the VA hospital in Jackson, Mississippi. The contract was for three years, although it could be extended. That wasn't bad, and the salary was also workable at $35,000 per year. However, the position entailed me supervising the residents on the general cardiovascular thoracic service. I was not looking for a job that was mostly supervisory. What's more, I wanted to enter cardiac surgery, not a program that included all three specialties including thoracic and vascular surgery.

Offers two and three on the list simply disappeared from our communication at some point in the process. A department head in Alexandria, Virginia, was supposed to call me back after talking with Dr. Najafi, but he did not. Similarly, the head of a multispecialty group in Wisconsin, who asked me not to accept a job offer anywhere else for three to four weeks, never even contacted me again.

That left a fourth option from a medical center in Bay City, Michigan. This offer was primarily in thoracic surgery, which was the first strike against it. But more worrisome was that each physician there had their own solo practice with no fixed salary. That meant competition with the other members, and everyone would be more senior than me. It also meant that I would not have loyalty to one hospital, and loyalty had always been—and would always be—very important to me. It may seem like an advantage to have flexibility to do cases in any hospital where you qualify, but I wanted to avoid this if at all possible. What if I did a case in one hospital, but while I was traveling to a second one, my first patient started to bleed? I would not want to rely on someone else to take care of my patient before I was able to return. This was why I always said I would rather do two cases in one hospital in a given day than three cases in three hospitals.

I was somewhat at a loss for what to do. I could imagine eventually having a practice where I was able to lecture and research and write about my cases—a wide variety of intellectual activities based on my own data. I had to settle down in surgery first, however, before I could worry about any of those things. But where?

This was when Providence would once again enter my life. I was still working with Dr. Najafi, having taken the position he offered as an adjunct attending, when one day he called to inform me that he had a letter on his desk. Apparently, a group in Connecticut was looking for a cardiac surgeon. Would I like to reach out to them?

Absolutely! At the time, it was a two-man group in private practice in Hartford, Connecticut. They performed primarily thoracic and vascular surgery, but they did do some cardiac surgery, and they were looking for a cardiac surgeon specifically to add more cardiac surgical volume. This group had a copy of the procedures I performed during my residency program and were impressed by my references, especially the one from Dr. Beattie.

In March 1976, I was asked to come and meet with the two partners in the doctor's lounge at St. Francis Hospital. Ranjana and I flew to Hartford and stayed in a hotel. The next day, I reached the doctor's lounge with plenty of time to spare, but nobody showed up. I waited there for a few hours, pondering my future. In the meantime, I had a conversation with a general surgeon, Dr. Youssef Horanieh, who gave me what felt like an objective evaluation of St. Francis. Finally, one of the partners showed up.

He apologized for being late, and for the other partner not showing up at all. But then he said, "Now I have to go home to have dinner with my family. I promised them I would be there." I could appreciate the desire to balance work and family, but I had come a long way and had been waiting patiently. *This is not going to end well*, I thought. But I agreed to stay an extra day.

The following day, however, my fortunes turned around. When I reached the office on Woodland Street, the partner I had not met the day before greeted me graciously. He shook my hand and offered me the job starting on July 9, immediately after the holiday. I do not recall any discussion regarding a contract or specifics like vacation time. He did mention that my salary would be $30,000 per year, which was commensurate with some of the other opportunities I had been exploring.

As I mentioned, the two-man team worked mainly in thoracic and vascular surgery practice, with some cardiac surgery. They covered many hospitals, including not only St. Francis and Mount Sinai in Hartford but also Rockville General Hospital, New Britain General Hospital, Bristol Hospital, the VA Hospital and the University of Connecticut. Neither of these factors made their office a perfect fit, but it was close enough for me to commit to making the most out of the situation.

I arrived in New England as a full-fledged surgeon, with Ranjana and Sujit accompanying me. It had been a long journey to get there, but I was resolved to make focused advancement in my chosen profession and area of specialization. I had come too far to let this golden opportunity pass me by. I was thirty-four years old.

Winning the inter-collegiate tournament as the captain of the tennis team at AIIMS; 1962

Receiving my medical degree from AIIMS; 1963

Official graduation photo from AIIMS; 1963

My big family sendoff to the U.S.; 1968

Surgical residents at Rochester General Hospital; 1969

Dr. Raymond Hinshaw, Chief of Surgery General Hospital, who gave me
my first job in 1968

My new wife, Ranjana, performing a tikka ceremony during our wedding in Allahabad; 1971

My mother attending my wedding ceremony in Allahabad; 1971

My father attending my wedding ceremony in Allahabad; 1971

Me in the dissection hall at Rush Medical College, Chicago; 1971

School children visiting Rush Medical College, Chicago; 1971

The faculty at Presbyterian-St. Luke's Hospital, Chicago; 1974

Dr. Hassan Najafi, Professor and Chairman of Cardiothoracic Surgery at Presbyterian-St. Luke's Hospital, Chicago; 1972

St. Francis Hospital and Medical Center, Hartford, Connecticut

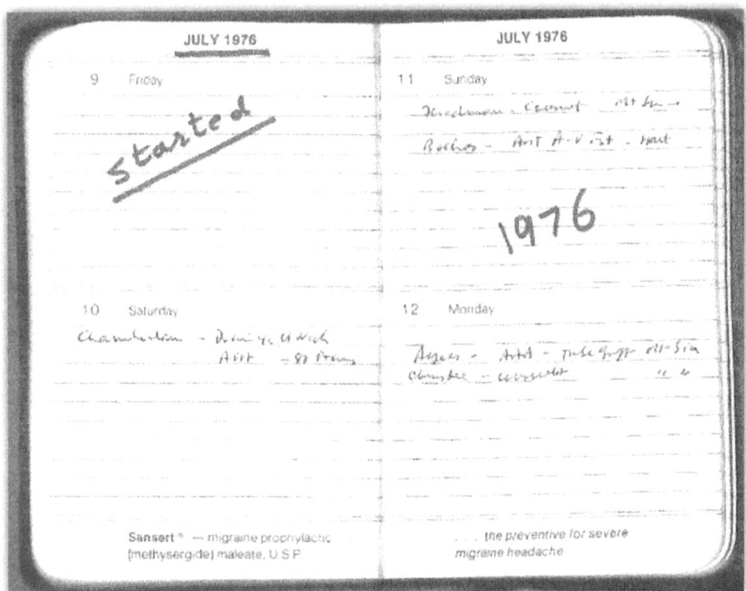

My daily diary of patients at St. Francis; 1976

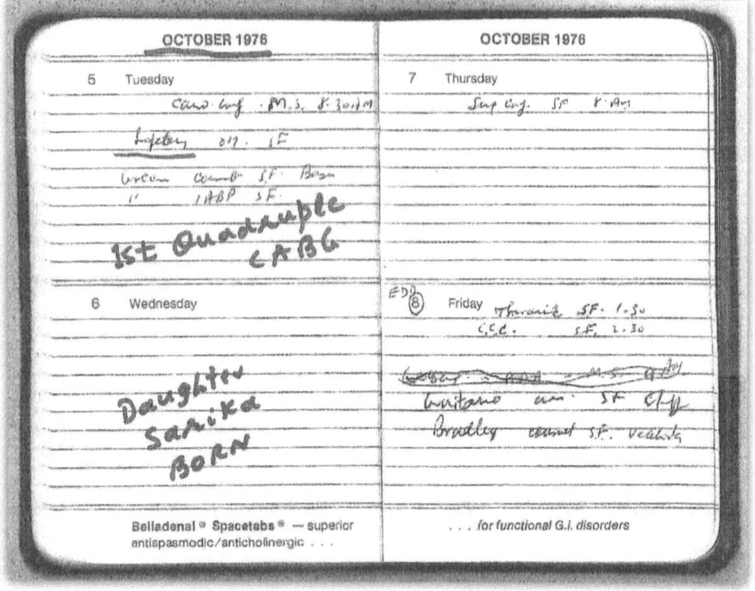

Marking my first quadruple bypass consult followed by the birth of my daughter, Sarika; 1976

Sister Francis Marie bids farewell to Mr. Madappa as Dr. Chawla (left) looks on.

Newspaper clip featuring my patient, Mr. Madappa, the executive secretary to the President of India, along with Sister Francis Marie; 1979

Me and my wife visiting Mr. Madappa after his open-heart surgery; President's residence, Rashtrapati Bhavan; circa 1980

Giving my son, Sujit, his first haircut, Chicago; 1973

Playing with my daughter, Sarika, West Hartford; 1984

Chapter Fourteen

In April of 1976, I got my license to practice in Connecticut. In June, I rented a condominium in Bloomfield, for $315 per month, and moved in with my family—which was growing, as my wife was now pregnant with our second child due to arrive in October.

On July 9, at Rockville Hospital, I started my clinical work with an AV fistula, a connection that is established between an artery and a vein for dialysis access. I also did what is known as a BMS (a bronchoscopy, mediastinoscopy, and scalene biopsy), as well as an independent abdominal aortic surgery at Mount Sinai Hospital.

It seemed my surgical career had begun unremarkably. Soon, however, the situation abruptly changed. My first cardiac consult was on Saturday, August 7. It was an emergency. The patient was a young male who presented with unstable angina and an angiogram showing an LAD critical stenosis. The LAD is the left anterior descending coronary artery, one of two branches of the left main coronary artery. The stenosis meant there was a narrowing of that artery that resulted in a significant reduction in blood-flow capacity. The treatment option for coronary angioplasty was not yet available at St. Francis Hospital.

The patient was taken to the operating room that Sunday. While he was being anesthetized, his blood pressure waxed and waned. As I recall, we had intravenous nitroglycerine for high blood pressure, norepinephrine for low blood pressure, and morphine as an anesthetic agent, with no availability of microdrips.

The patient then went into cardiac arrest before we could even start the surgical procedure. We performed external cardiac massage, placed him on a cardiopulmonary bypass via his groin, and proceeded to complete the procedure. Tragically, the patient could not come off the bypass and died on the operating table.

It was a shock. A new cardiac surgeon in town, performing only a single bypass surgery, and the patient dies on the operating table? I had done many such cases in my training, and far more complicated cases as well, including double and triple bypasses. I had applied the same level of mental focus to the procedure that I had brought first to my schooling and then to my training. But the team was not in sync or properly prepared as to what our steps would be.

I did some soul searching after the event. I realized it could have been the end of my career. But the referring cardiologist, Dr. Arthur Landry, trusted me enough to continue with the other three cardiac patients for whom I had already consulted.

One was a closed mitral commissurotomy, a surgery that helps improve blood flow through one of the heart valves, in this case the mitral valve. The second was a double bypass surgery. Both procedures went well, which settled my anxiety.

That left a fourth patient, a coronary artery disease patient who would require quadruple coronary artery bypass grafting. I had never done a four-vessel bypass in my training. It was not a common procedure done by the residents; as a longer and more difficult case, it was reserved for attending physicians only. I had just gone through a patient dying on the operating-room table with a single vessel disease. In addition, my wife had just gone through an emergency appendectomy and was due to deliver our baby any day now.

To quell my nerves, I decided to have a rehearsal of the steps of the procedure with the newly formed cardiac team, including a dedicated cardiac anesthesiologist. I wanted to stress what my needs would be, including the all-important point of myocardial preservation. Together, we rehearsed our steps, going over the cardiopulmonary setup by perfusionist Wally Wohlfert in great detail. When I was finally satisfied that our extensive preparations had been completed, I went home.

Luckily, the quadruple bypass procedure went very well, and the next day, on October 6, my wife delivered our beautiful baby girl, Sarika. In honor of the successful operation, the patient became a family friend, and we often invited him to my daughter's birthday parties! He wrote a very complimentary letter to the CEO of St. Francis, Sister Francis Marie Garvey, thanking all the people involved in his care.

After my first case, I thought my career might be over, but by my fourth case, I knew I could succeed in health care—provided I never took for granted the responsibility of bringing my greatest mental focus to my work.

Speaking of Sister Francis Marie, she was in charge of overseeing the entire hospital. One of her special interests was to reinvigorate the open-heart surgery program at St. Francis Hospital. In addition to our group, there were two other teams who worked at St. Francis as well.

The original team was led by Dr. Harold Knight and Dr. Al Gambrini. Dr. Knight had started the open-heart surgery department at St. Francis Hospital during the days of rheumatic heart disease, when patients used to arrive for medical or surgical evaluation very late in the progression of their ailments.

Most of the very sick patients were then transferred to Brigham and Women's Hospital in Boston under Dr. Larry Cohen, or to Hartford Hospital. After the sudden unexpected death of Dr. Knight, Dr. Gambrini sought to preserve the team through various options but was unsuccessful.

At that point, Sister Francis Marie invited a team headed by Dr. Henry Low to come over from Hartford Hospital. That team was still working there when I arrived. All of them were excellent surgeons, but because Hartford Hospital was their primary hospital, their timing was unpredictable. As was related to me by many St. Francis Hospital cardiologists, one did not know with any certainty when the members of this team would be arriving at their operations or to supervise postoperative care. Our team, by contrast, was able to provide 24/7 care of our patients. While

Dr. Low's team came when they had time, we had established a highly effective routine by the end of 1976 and early 1977. This caused Dr. Low to reconsider his relationship with St. Francis, at one point mentioning, "Since St. Francis has their own cardiac surgeon now, we can go back to Hartford Hospital."

Dr. Low also became my mentor to discuss difficult cases. We had at least two meetings, with him asking if I could join his team so they could have a larger group to cover the whole Hartford market. He would be in charge at Hartford Hospital while I would stay in charge at St. Francis Hospital. For a variety of reasons, this did not materialize. After Low's team left and Dr. Gambrini's team did not succeed, we were the only ones left at St. Francis Hospital. From that point on, our confidence grew.

In 1977, I signed my first contract with Cardiovascular and Thoracic Associates LLC. My salary was increased almost three-fold to $96,000. I was promised one-third partnership after five years with all the benefits that would entail, including an equal voice in business affairs, becoming an equal shareholder, and being appointed director. Any way you looked at it, my career was definitely on the upswing.

ð

Chapter Fifteen

For the next decade, I entered what might be called "the settling period." During this time, we grew a stable team of surgeons and oversaw a significant increase in the number of referrals. There were many factors that contributed to our growth. One was working closely with the other physicians on the staff at St. Francis Hospital. Early on in my practice, I met a primary care physician at a medical meeting. He told me that he sent all his cardiac patients to Hartford Hospital. His only issue was that when he sent a patient there, they never came back to him because the local cardiologist took over their care.

I told him, "We are here to take care of your patient for the next eight to ten days. This patient belongs to you. We will keep in touch with you whether there is good or bad news, and together, we will take care of the patient. If the patient needs a follow-up EKG or an echocardiogram, we will call you first."

It was this attitude that established our reputation for humility and openness at St. Francis. I also made sure to maintain a simple philosophy of performing only one case per day, unless there was an emergency. I wanted to be able to take the best care of the patient that I could during the immediate postoperative phase, including placing phone calls to the family, the internist, and the cardiologist. Many days, I didn't even leave the premises while the patient emerged from surgery. I would even bring my lunch from home so I could be prepared for any eventuality.

The number of cardiac catheterization procedures were increasing at the nearby hospital, Mount Sinai Hospital, with Dr. Arthur Riba as the chief of cardiology. These were busy days, with covering the operating room in the morning, postoperative care in the afternoon with new patients after their cardiac catheterization at St. Francis Hospital, then consulting new patients at Mount Sinai Hospital, which was getting busier every day.

I wasn't always home to see my children during the week—leaving the house before they woke up and coming home after their dinnertime. They commented that they didn't see me often, and that made me feel regretful but I worked hard to make it up over the weekends. I made it a point to attend every school concert and soccer and baseball games, and we regularly went out to dinner as a family.

During this settling period, we hired some new surgeons for our practice. I did not advertise for these individuals. I did not want to interview ten people for a single position. Instead, I went to the places of my previous training, to my colleagues who ran residency programs, and asked them, "Who is the best surgeon that you have?" I would let them choose the candidate for me, because they knew how good that doctor was, and then I would set up the interview. Several of my new hires stood out among all the others—those who could withstand the pressures of the profession and were loyal through every situation.

Dr. Stuart Houser was the first surgeon we hired in 1978, when our cardiac surgical volume hit two hundred cases. He was from my alma mater, Rochester General Hospital, where I finished my general surgery residency. He had excellent credentials. He was very hard working and trustworthy. He was also eager to perform surgery on high-risk patients, such as when a coronary artery bypass graft had to be redone in a patient. In the very unfortunate situation where a patient died in the operating room, Dr. Houser would lament over the person's passing. But he also wanted to know, *Why did this patient die? Why did the heart muscle die?* He was always thinking. This was the start of his developing interest in pathology and his research at the University of Connecticut in ischemic hearts (hearts that have reduced blood flow and thus reduced oxygen). Once he was satisfied with his career as a cardiac surgeon, he chose to leave the practice to pursue "the love of his life": to be a resident in pathology at Massachusetts General Hospital. He finished his board certification in that area on his first attempt, and published the book *The Operated Heart at Autopsy.*

Dr. Fayyaz Hashmi joined our group in 1982 and was our resident in general surgery at St. Francis Hospital. He came to our team after completing his cardiac and thoracic residency at the University of Kentucky Medical Center. We knew that

Dr. Hashmi was an excellent surgical technician along with being a caring physician, eager to tackle new technologies. We worked together for the next thirteen years until he returned to Pakistan, where he developed a flourishing cardiac center. He came back for a short time in early 2000, helping the team. He was one of my loyal partners, and we sometimes reflected on how close we had become—a Hindu and a Muslim—and how different that situation was from the days of the Partition when I was just a boy. Sincerity and loyalty can truly trump imagined political and religious differences.

Dr. Tim Lehman was the fourth surgeon we hired. He had just finished his training in cardiothoracic surgery. I was sitting in my office when a young person walked in and said, "I have just finished my training, and I'm looking for a job." Once he was hired, he went on to excel in developing electrophysiological specialties for the group.

Fast forward to 1995, when we hired Dr. Arshad Quadri. He was a hard worker and a team player. His mind was also working on inventing new technologies to make operations easier, and he developed the percutaneous mitral valve replacement. He also developed thoracic aortic aneurysm surgery. He eventually joined another team, but we have remained good friends since.

These men were my backbone, through all the travails that would come to our practice. We shared a common philosophy, one that Dr. Houser spoke of when he eventually retired in 1996. In his final address to the staff, he cited some of his favorite maxims that had consciously and unconsciously informed our organization for many years, including:

Things don't just happen; one makes things happen.
If you do good work, the patient will come.
There is a rattlesnake in every gulch.
Be honest with yourself, your colleagues, and your patients.

It was indeed, as Dr. Houser stated, a great advantage to work in a group who shared the same philosophy of patient care and demand for personal excellence.

I should mention that we required help from other specialties, especially the pulmonary department. Dr. Bamalin Lahiri was chief of the Pulmonary and Critical Care Department, and he managed most of my patients if they required pulmonary support. His greatest quality was that he was available 24/7 for consultation.

In this work, it is crucial to have trusted and loyal professionals in other capacities. Mr. Howard Case was the chartered public accountant with our group, and he became my fast friend. Over the next forty-plus years of my surgical career, he would help me in more ways than I could count. It was also critical to have my own trusted lawyer, Mr. Steve Miller, to advise me on all matters.

Perhaps the most important nonmedical member to have on the team is a secretary who is efficient, pleasant with patients, honest, and loyal. Our first secretary, Barbara (Bettencourt) Dunbar, was working for a busy, full-time cardiologist, Dr. David O'Reily, when I met her. She greeted every patient with respect and helped them in any way they needed. In addition to her wonderful personality, she had great skills as well. She was thoroughly organized and could locate anything you might need in a flash. She also excelled at transcription, including those passages that involved complex medical terminology. She eventually transitioned from receptionist to business manager, and we worked well together for five years before she started raising her family. She rejoined us a few years later and worked with us until my retirement.

The second person I hired was Susan (Vernelli) Pereslugoff, initially as a nurse and later as a business manager. When I first went to interview Susan, she was working in the pulmonary critical care unit at the hospital. She kept me waiting while she prepared a patient's bed and made them as comfortable as she could, checking their nutrition, vital signs, and overall comfort level. She did not stop her work to meet with me, which showed that her dedication was to the patient first and everything else came later.

The third person I hired was Sandy Mitchell, who was working for Dr. Robert Cohen, a cardiologist with whom I had a constant communication. The way she treated everyone, patients and doctors alike, made all of us feel at ease and cared for. Following Dr. Cohen's death, Sandy became available. I knew our interview would be cursory from my end because I was already convinced of her great value. She was so nervous, however, that she spilled her coffee! Of course I hired her, and all three of these women stayed with my group for two to three decades. I did my best to help them provide for their families and themselves.

Chapter Sixteen

According to the available information, St. Francis Hospital performed 75 open-heart surgeries in 1975. That number increased to 136 in 1976 and 197 in 1977. We had a goal of treating 200 patients per year—a goal we accomplished and celebrated in 1978, thanking the entire team for their effort. From then on, the volume of surgeries grew by 40 or 50 patients per year and was anticipated to be 500 in the year 1983.

Simultaneously, publicity surrounding our efforts was increasing. In the August 14, 1977 issue of the *Hartford Courant*, David Rhinelander wrote: "The demand for open-heart surgery in the city has expanded to the point that St. Francis Hospital now has its own team of surgeons. St. Francis is averaging three to four operations per week and will soon have the capacity to expand to six to eight cases."

Patients were now traveling to Hartford to have their procedures performed by our team, some from as far away as India. When Kondendera Mandappa, the personal secretary to the then president of India, Neelam Sanjiva Reddy, suffered a heart attack at the age of fifty-eight, he developed a left ventricular aneurysm. He was referred to our team by Dr. Beattie—the same man whose letter had helped get me this job in the first place—for resection of the left ventricular aneurysm and coronary artery bypass grafting. One patient came from as far away as Syria for coronary bypass grafting, after having been referred by Dr. Joseph Hanna.

But perhaps our most famous patient was Governor William A. O'Neill of Connecticut who was sworn in December 31, 1980.

In late March 1981, less than two months after the former governor Ella Grasso had passed away from a painful and agonizing battle with cancer, the new governor complained of coughing spells which he attributed to smoking three packs of cigarettes per day. When he was visiting Germany, he had shortness of breath while trying to climb to a castle. Later, he was touring southern Connecticut for work, and he had chest pains during minimal activity.

The governor was seen by his primary care physician, John Rixon, followed by his cardiologist. But it wasn't until Dr. Robert Jeresaty—chief of cardiology at St. Francis—performed cardiac catheterization on the governor, that it revealed two-vessel coronary artery disease (CAD), a critical condition. More than one CAD was considered a surgical candidate at that time. Because he was experiencing angina at rest, the governor was scheduled to undergo double coronary artery bypass grafting (CABG) at St. Francis. The operation was set for December 4, 1981.

This was the chance for me to prove my philosophy of treating every patient the same, whether VIP or a regular patient. After the skin is cut, once you go down deep into the body, everyone is the same; their blood is red, and it all runs in the same direction. Whether they were an average person or the governor of the state, when that patient was on my operating table, I saw God in them. It was something my mother taught me from a very young age. That was why I never took a shortcut, no matter what. If there was a space between sutures that I knew would later cause that area to bleed, I added another stitch. Every operation had to be perfect from my side. Then, after I had done everything I could do, I would leave the rest up to my prayers.

Fortunately, the governor had the ideal anatomy for a bypass surgery, with normal heart function, excellent distal runoff (a measure of blood flow, an important factor in the success of vascular grafts), and a good saphenous vein. The success of Gov. O'Neill's surgery hit the front page of the *Hartford Courant* and in *The New York Times*. The publicity was a boost to the image of cardiac surgery at St. Francis Hospital. It was also covered by *India Today*, which sometimes ran Indian success stories from abroad. I recall being at a Christmas party one night, and the Indian publisher of that magazine called to ask me a few questions. When the issue reached back home, my whole family saw it, and they spread the news. I, the youngest child of a family who was forcibly relocated after the Partition, had become a surgeon who operated on such famous people as a United States governor!

After his operation, the governor and his wife, Nikki, became our friends. I considered myself fortunate to go to his house for a cup of coffee or to eat his wife's cooking. I wondered later what caused Gov. O'Neill to choose St. Francis Hospital to care for his illness rather than bigger centers like those that existed in New York or Boston. His primary care physician was attached to St. Francis, but that alone wouldn't have been enough to guarantee his coming to our team for his needs. Our cardiac team was well established.

Perhaps it was Providence that led to one of the highlights of my career? I still recall it fondly, especially as the next several years would prove to contain challenges of a kind I could never have predicted.

Chapter Seventeen

By 1984, we had a team of six surgeons at St. Francis Hospital, performing more than eight hundred cases that year. At this juncture, we were the only team of cardiac surgeons operating in the hospital, and our facility was not coping well with the demand. We did not have enough operating-room staff or support staff, so St. Francis could only accommodate eight patients per week. This meant that we had eight to ten patients awaiting surgery in-house at any given time. Meanwhile, an additional forty patients were waiting at home for an average of two months for elective open-heart surgery. When we had a highly unfortunate event, where one patient died at home waiting for his coronary bypass surgery, it seemed to signal to some that we needed more than one team of surgeons.

Not having more than one team of surgeons was not the main problem, however. Neither was the concern of some cardiologists that with only one team, there was no one available to consult with for a second opinion. We had three different surgeons on our team that a patient could consult with for such a second pair of eyes. I was summoned to give a presentation to the newly appointed chief of surgery. I said I was completely agreeable to having a second team that could relieve our tension as well as provide a second opinion, manpower for extra cases, and competition. I did inquire whether the timing was right, but that was the only resistance I offered.

In retrospect, I'm not sure that what I said would have mattered much. Our experience with the chief of surgery went poorly from the beginning. Whenever we requested a budgetary item, it was automatically denied. We had planned an organized expansion that accounted for every service, including surgeons, perfusionists, operating-room nurses, and intensive care nurses. But the chief of surgery stopped the addition of two extra beds during our renovation plans. What it all came down to, I believe, was that he felt cardiac surgery was progressing too fast for the facility to handle, and he was trying to make every effort to contain us.

We continued our good work, nonetheless. By now, we also had the services of Dr. Kishan Tandon, a general surgeon who was kind enough to help us during our surgical procedures. Incredibly enough, he had been my classmate back in our premedical studies in Delhi from 1958 to 1959! We lost touch after going to different medical schools, but he found his way to Hartford. When we were introduced, we knew the other person looked familiar—and from that time on, we worked together extensively. In addition to his own practice, Dr. Tandon assisted me in open-heart surgery for the next twenty-five years. He helped us on both routine and complicated cases. I always had a feeling of calm whenever we were able to work together because he always knew what kind of help I needed. We truly knew each other's moves during an operation to the point that he instinctively knew all my steps and how to provide the best veins for bypass surgery. In fact, one of the anesthesiologists made the statement that "watching the two of you work together is like watching a symphony."

Debbie Winter, our operating-room technician, also knew all my procedures intimately, as she had been present since the beginning of the open-heart program. Debbie was always two steps ahead of me, and if I was struggling with an issue such as bleeding, she always had the right instrument ready in her hand without me having to ask for it.

Much later, we hired Roxanne Mongeone as our first private physician's assistant (PA). She was quiet but extremely competent as a surgeon's assistant. Later, we were lucky to have Pat Cosgrove as the lead PA. Pat received the utmost support from his colleagues, and he is still providing the same level of service today.

As I mentioned earlier, you need a consistent team to have the best results. With my team, I was able to enjoy each and every case, and the feeling extended throughout our surgical unit, from the operating room to the office.

At that time, every one of our surgeons was doing every kind of procedure, including cardiac surgery, vascular surgery, thoracic surgery, and AV fistulas for dialysis patients. I suggested to my senior partner that we should have a few surgeons who specialized in heart surgery. That way, we could compete with any potential new second team of cardiac surgeons that might come in.

These discussions proved fruitless over a period of nearly six months, during which my senior partner and I went back and forth. There was little support around the idea of increasing the infrastructure of St. Francis to accommodate the increase in volume.

I became so disheartened that I even visited other institutions in case our relationship broke down completely. That was my motto after all—always have a second option. *Could I survive if I had to go out on my own?* I visited different hospitals around the state, seeing the quality of the care they offered and talking with different surgeons and members of their support staff. I wondered, *Could I survive in competition with the team I had already built?* But that was not at all what I wanted to do.

What I wanted to do was reiterate that our group wished to focus on cardiac surgery, and we were ready to walk away if that wish was not granted. My senior partner's response was, "As long as I am here, everyone will perform every kind of surgery." He indicated that my reputation would suffer if we separated.

I did not know how he could believe there was any threat to my reputation. All of our cardiology consults were coming to us because of our reputations. Not only did cardiologists know us, but the family members of everyone whom we had operated on successfully were referring new patients by word-of-mouth. I did not want to leave, but I knew that my reputation would be fine if I chose to do so.

Chapter Eighteen

Throughout the tumultuous years that ensued, I tried my best to concentrate solely on patient care. Whereas I used to make two patient rounds, morning and evening, now I made three rounds. I did not want anything to appear out of line. If there was a patient issue, I was there to take care of it. This commitment had begun years ago with my intention not to do surgeries at multiple hospitals in the same day, and it continued now with my availability to take care of any complications.

In 1984, Dr. Houser, Dr. Hashmi, and I split from the larger group. We officially incorporated on March 1, 1984, as a private entity named Cardiac Surgeons PC with surgical privileges at St. Francis Hospital. The three of us made up the board of directors. None of us took a salary for the first several months. Instead, we put in our own seed money, as we had no cash flow. In this way, we were able to cover the cost of salaries for our secretaries and expenses for insurance and materials, such as dressings and gloves.

I vividly remember this time as a period of competition, productivity, growth, politics, and survival. Members of the hospital administration who were against us went so far as to say that the cardiac program would never grow and was in fact nothing more than "a flash in the pan." These individuals could not have been more wrong, as the volume of cases continued to increase exponentially.

It was clear to me that St. Francis had become an established institution for open-heart surgery. We were accepting more high-risk patients than ever before, such as those who required intra-aortic balloon pumps, a device that helps your heart pump more blood. We were also becoming very well known for our work in early cardiac catheterization for acute myocardial infarction patients (which is another way of saying those who had had a heart attack). Our referral base had increased from Hartford County to initially include Rockville General Hospital and Manchester Memorial Hospital, then Bakus Hospital in Norwich and Lawrence and Memorial Hospital in New London. Getting transfers from so many other locations increased the reputation of our hospital as well as its revenue; we were not only trusted surgeons but also surgeons trusted with the post-operative care of patients. Our facilities had progressed to the point where the chief of cardiology at the University of Connecticut had requested our support for their cardiac catheterization program.

Our success inflamed our detractors. It was clear to me that my former senior partner viewed us as disloyal for splitting from the team. The chief of surgery's motivations were harder to parse. He was a full-time employee of the hospital, so why would he be competing with us? My struggles with these two individuals over the next three years made a quadruple bypass surgery seem easy! All jokes aside, it was an extraordinarily difficult time. I was the recipient of so much scrutiny that without honest hard work and faith, I could not have survived.

One formal complaint after another was lodged against me. I was cited for misusing the operating-room guidelines—and even convincing a triage physician to change his perspective in order to accommodate my wishes. I was censured for not following the institution's triage policy and for unethical conduct; I was warned that further violation would be forwarded to the Ethics Committee of the Hartford County Medical Association. For over two years, I fought to clear my name from this event, and, ultimately, I was successful.

At that time, due to a lack of space and staffing on the weekends, St. Francis Hospital was forced to reduce surgical activities on those days except in dire emergencies. In one case, a patient with uremic pericardial effusion was having problems with hypotension during hemodialysis on a Friday. He was transferred to intensive care. Because the operating room was busy on Saturday, he was operated upon on Sunday and was saved. I was accused of operating on the patient too soon, with the chief of surgery believing it could have waited for the following week. It was only after I obtained a note from the renal consultant (as this was a kidney-related matter) and a note from the operating room supervisor, both of whom averred that this was in fact an emergency—and that they had requested the case be performed on a Sunday morning, with satisfactory outcomes—that this particular harassment stopped.

Another patient, a sixty-one-year-old male at University of Connecticut, had cardiac catheterization for unstable angina and revealed 99 percent blockage of his left main coronary artery and 80 percent narrowing of the right coronary artery. Following catheterization, the patient had a hypotensive episode. He arrived on Saturday evening and was operated on successfully on Sunday morning. It was again cited that there was no documentation indicating the necessity for performing this procedure as an emergency on a weekend. Only after obtaining four letters from different cardiologists did I receive acknowledgement that the patient was a bona fide emergency, and the case was closed.

But the mean-spirited nature of the persecution continued. More emergency cases performed on weekends were investigated. Forget about the fact that these operations were successful; I was being called to account simply for a lack of documentation indicating the necessity for scheduling these procedures as an emergency. In essence, I was accused of misrepresenting or "shading" the details of the case to abuse the system and perform my surgeries too soon. Then I was told that continuing to do so "could result in your being asked to appear before the medical staff council to explain chronic violation of the established operating room policy."

With each accusation, the chief of surgery would back down without ever apologizing. He would simply say that after further examination, he considered this particular case closed.

Meanwhile, the amount of energy and effort that went into defending my good name was taking away from my proper focus, which should have been patient care. It took time to get letters of support from whoever happened to have the greatest knowledge of a particular case. All just because the chief was after me to get anything he could use to take my surgical privileges away.

Nonetheless, I learned many lessons from this series of unfortunate events. For example, it became a practice of mine not to leave any letter unanswered on my desk, especially if it involved my integrity, ethics, or reputation. I replied every time, giving a detailed picture and supplying documents from every person with knowledge of the case. And, of course, because there were no complaints about patient care—the ultimate matter to which we had all supposedly devoted our lives—I would always be found to be in the right at the end of the day. No matter how exhausting that process turned out to be.

Chapter Nineteen

In addition to the false and misleading charges that were being leveled against me, our team faced challenges in other areas as well. One of these had to do with scheduling, which is far more important in the surgical field than it might immediately seem. Our team was consistently doing 66 percent of the cases while getting only 50 percent of the morning slots. Most people who are familiar with the medical environment know that getting operated on in the morning is better. Surgeons are sharper; nurses are more attuned. Even more relevant to our team was the fact that if there was a shortage of beds, the afternoon cases were the most likely to be canceled.

Unfortunately, this was not the only challenge I was dealing with. Our team had also been placed on the "nonteaching service," meaning we would not be able to assist in the education of young residents, nor would we be able to benefit from the assistance of those residents during our own surgical operations. In a special communique, we were told that unless we showed increased improvement in the teaching of the residents, including attendance at all meetings, we would stay in the nonteaching service. Our team sent a letter back outlining the problem from our perspective, which was a lack of paramedical help given the growing cardiac surgery volume. Simply put, we had not been provided with enough physician assistants. Therefore, we were the ones who had to take the patient's history and do their physicals, administer everything pre- and post-op, and do a host of other jobs, including things as basic but necessary as pulling out chest tubes.

Finally, after all the attempts to sabotage my team and me, I had had enough. On June 14th, 1984, I wrote a letter to Sister Francis Marie, the CEO of the hospital, regarding the future of cardiac surgery at St. Francis. As CEO, she was not a very forbidding presence. You would see her walking around the hospital very quietly, greeting patients and their families. Yet deep down, she knew everything about the hospital. I had kept in close contact with her before, but now I felt I had to outline the number and the scope of the problems we were experiencing.

My letter to Sister Francis Marie detailed everything, including the lack of enthusiasm for successful cardiac surgery, the jockeying of the beds and who was permitted morning operating room slots, and the lack of support that landed us in the nonteaching service. I also described my rebuffed attempts to reach the chief of surgery to discuss these matters; instead he installed his secretaries as a wall in front of our attempts to communicate. I asked for Sister Francis Marie's support and expressed my concerns that this treatment would eventually lead to our team being cut loose from the hospital.

I went to see her in person as a follow-up to my letter. She kept her responses brief, but at the same time, she was thoroughly reassuring.

"Dr. Chawla," she told me. "Don't worry about anything. Before the chief can do anything, he has to come to me."

I felt heartened by Sister Francis Marie's words. I had always believed that if I did honest work within the rules—for my patients, their families, our cardiologists, and our referring internists—that I would survive. I had responded to every communication about my ethics, as I mentioned, but I had also kept my surgical staff informed of everything—as well as my private lawyer. And now, I had brought the CEO of the hospital into the loop as well.

When there was nothing else for me to do tactically, I prayed. I have prayed daily for as long as I can remember. My mother taught me how to pray—and even more importantly, how to keep praying—every day, every hour of the day, often when I don't even know I'm doing it. This meant that any time an issue came up, I was able to sit and concentrate on it for as long as the situation required, as my faculties were already predisposed in this direction.

This ability to collect myself became important as the political situation came to a head. I learned that the director of the surgical intensive care unit was wrongly spreading rumors about my mental health. Around the same time, on June 25, 1987, my beloved mother died. I was expected to go to India to participate in the last rites and cremation, and to immerse her ashes in the river Ganges. To add to the strain, I was in the middle of preparing to study for the Board recertification examination.

When my mother passed away, I never felt like she was taken away from me. I never felt that I would miss her presence, for I knew she was with me, watching over me, from another plane. Nonetheless, I had to travel back to India to do my filial duty. There is a local ceremony at home where the person's body is laid out on the floor, not the bed or the cot. After the priest administers the last prayers, the body goes to the cremation ground, which had to be done on the same day before sundown. With my flight to India taking twenty-four hours, I knew I would not be able to arrive in time, but I would be there with the family to spread her ashes in the river Ganges. This is where the priest records the family genealogy for generations. There you could see members of the Chawla family who had died fifty years ago, one hundred years ago, or even earlier.

I was in a real quandary as to what to do. Often when such situations have occurred in my life, I have turned to my wife, Ranjana. In addition to all her wonderful qualities, she has always been a very helpful sounding board, and she has never been afraid to speak her own opinion as an independent person looking in.

I asked her what she thought about this thorny situation. She advised me that the most important thing I could do was to fulfill my filial duty toward my mother. The next most important thing was for me to study, pass my examinations, and thereby protect my livelihood. The politics were the least important thing for me to attend to—in part, because they were not going to go away. I did not need to stay in America to protect my name but could deal with whatever I needed to when I returned.

I took Ranjana's advice, with one addendum. In order to stop the rumors from spreading during my absence, before leaving for India, I met with the physician who had started them. I said to him, "Hi, I heard you have been spreading rumors about my mental stability. Are those people wrong, and you never said that? Or did you say that and are you sorry for it? Or did you say it and mean it? Whatever the case, I would suggest you stop. I have to go home to attend my mother's funeral, but if you continue to libel me, you will hear from my lawyer."

After that, I never heard anything about him spreading rumors behind my back ever again.

Chapter Twenty

From the day of my mother's death, I have always felt that she was in the company of the gods, and she was with me, helping me every day of my life. And I would need that help, because my challenges at the hospital were not going away. The next year, when a cardiac surgery task force was organized, our team members were not invited. How could such a unique committee, recommended by the board to address the clinical activities of the cardiac surgery program, make any headway without our input? The only area-physician representation came from a thoracic surgeon from the other team. He was supposed to inform us of the proceedings, but we did not receive the reports until after their completion.

The challenges this task force faced were real. They were attempting to address matters such as the excessive length of preoperative stays, the increase in weekend emergencies, and the significant number of transfers from other hospitals, all of which created confusion and a significant number of agitated patients and families who had been bumped off the schedule. But the problem, in my opinion, lay in one area specifically: the sheer increase in the volume of patients. Therefore, there should have been a straightforward solution consisting of a number of changes: hiring more nurses, opening more beds, keeping the quality of patient care high, and increasing revenues for the hospital. Instead, it appeared the whole task force meeting was about how to control the growth of our program. I could not understand why a full-service hospital would not commit its resources to become a premier cardiac surgery center. Why was this not "in our mission," as we were being told?

And then, all of a sudden, the tide started to turn. In 1988, the chief of surgery announced he was retiring. Upon hearing this, I took a moment to think back over the last four years of my life. They had been by far the hardest I had endured professionally. It was the perfect storm of misery, but now that storm started to abate. In January 1989, we welcomed the appointment of Dr. David D'Eramo as the new CEO of St. Francis Hospital.

Prior to his arrival, St. Francis Hospital had always been run by nuns. Sister Francis Marie, of whom I have spoken so highly, was the last layperson to run the hospital; as kind and insightful as she was, she may not have had the instinct to help St. Francis Hospital evolve into a top-tier institution. Instead, we seemed content with a static level of growth that left us always in the shadow of Hartford Hospital. The experience with Dr. D'Eramo, however, would prove to be quite different. He turned out to be the right person at the right time, a man who liked people and wanted to help them while also being deeply committed to the productivity of St. Francis.

I composed a letter to our new CEO, welcoming him to the hospital and introducing him to our group of doctors. Our team had been practicing there for the past twelve and half years—how time had flown, I realized, as I wrote that! Of course, I brought up the fact that we had earned a well-deserved reputation as one of the premier cardiac centers in Connecticut. Finally, I offered to meet with him in person in the near future to discuss our common goals.

At the time, I only gave him a small amount of information. Perhaps I was gun-shy from all the political storms I had weathered over the past four years. I felt it was prudent to wait to see how he would process the status of the cardiac program at the hospital before I said too much. But when I went to see him for the first time in March of that year—what a relief! I felt he was listening to me very carefully. He was interested in learning more about our program and had a very positive attitude. I still felt I should take a wait-and-see attitude, but we shared some very important touch points, such as the financial implications of the cardiac program for the growth of the hospital, and the deleterious impact of long surgical wait times on both patient health and patient satisfaction.

When we discussed the first of these matters, the facts were pretty clear. At this time, cardiothoracic service was forecasted to be the top income producer at St. Francis, followed by general surgery, cardiology obstetrics, and gynecology.

The potential of the open-heart surgery program to fuel the bottom line for the hospital was, on the one hand, a very practical concern. This is an aspect of hospital care that any visionary leader must take into account, even though discussing the profit of one program versus another can be tricky—because, of course, we all want to help all patients. But when the financial implications of the growth of the cardiac program were combined with our team's genuine desire to help people, it became a no-brainer. This latter fact was communicated viscerally to Dr. D'Eramo through the statistics of how many cardiac patients were being forced to wait for their surgeries, some for a very long time at the hospital, while others were dying at home in the absence of critical care.

When Dr. D'Eramo saw these numbers, he couldn't believe his eyes, and it was one of the chief factors that motivated him to elevate me to levels of leadership where I could make more of an impact. If, before this meeting, I wasn't sure which way his leadership would lean—whether he would be following the same principles as before or heading off in a new direction—I now knew for certain that he understood me and saw what our team could do. I had connected with him somehow.

Chapter Twenty-One

Life at St. Francis had definitively turned around for the better. Dr. D'Eramo invited me, along with select other key physicians, to attend an executive retreat, and the whole concept gave me the feeling of a family unit working together. I felt a commitment and loyalty toward the progress of St. Francis Hospital and Medical Center, its values and future programs, such as I had not experienced in years.

This upswing was experienced on all fronts of my professional life. There was an increase in the number of operating-room slots our team was given. We were also approached by Dr. Arthur Riba, the chief of cardiology, who wrote to me, "Depending on your schedule, and if it is acceptable, I would like to send my first-year cardiology fellow to rotate with you on your cardiothoracic and vascular service. The experience of cardiology fellows to date has been a resounding success. I thank you and your colleagues in advance."

We seemed to be a functional hospital again, and the credit was largely due to Dr. D'Eramo. As CEO, he was focused, intelligent, and devoted to the cause of advancing St. Francis. That did not mean he was always an easy person to deal with. If he suspected you were not good at your work, or you were not fully invested in it, he would notice it. But if you were good, he would give all his strength to you.

The next year, I was given what I considered to be a very high honor. I was invited to be on the board of St. Francis Hospital. I was placed on both the Strategic and Planning Committee and the Quality Committee. At first, I did not know how to behave in such environments of executive leadership. I thought I was there to contribute my thoughts on cardiac surgery. So if they were talking about trauma, for example, I would just sit quietly, believing that was not my area of expertise. Someone from the administration, with whom I became friendly, took me aside and kindly informed me, "You are here to take care of the whole hospital, not just the cardiac department." Upon realizing that, I began sharing my ideas more freely with the other board members.

My lifelong commitment to patient care was now paying off. My whole life, I had asked myself a few simple questions when considering a new procedure or policy. *What will the patient's experience be? What do they need or want to see happen in a particular situation? What would the family need or want?* Coming from that perspective, many things became simple; it was easier for me to step into a leadership role because those were the principles I was leading on behalf of. It turns out I enjoyed my board work very much as a complement to my practice of medicine, and I am still on the Quality Committee all these years later.

Soon thereafter, Dr. D'Eramo began a hospital-wide initiative entitled "Planning for the Year 2000." He wrote to me:

Dear Sandy,

The vision of SFH in the year 2000 calls for the creation of centers of excellence beginning with a focus on the heart and on cancer. Clinical program management is a web of critical tasks, management systems, human resources, and organizational culture. It is a tool whose purpose is to assist SFH in developing better product delineation, packaging, and marketing.

You have been appointed to the Clinical Program Task Force on Heart Disease. Together, we will design the most appropriate structure and process for managing these clinical services; therefore, the responsibility of the success of this project is ours collectively.

I took his compliments and trust to heart. I began considering our entire department with a wide-angle lens. It was amazing what one could think about accomplishing when the road was freed of obstacles. Why couldn't we hire a cardiac surgeon of national fame, for example? Or have a separate administrator solely in charge of the operating rooms? Why couldn't we hire a full-time cardiac intensivist, to look after critically ill patients who came to us with complications from both cardiovascular diseases and other serious heart conditions? Or have anesthesiologists dedicated solely to cardiac surgery?

Not only could the personnel be enhanced, but the facilities could be expanded as well, whether in terms of adding new operating rooms or additional stepdown beds (for patients who still need a high level of care but who no longer have full intensive care needs). The technology could likewise be upgraded, including the use of lasers and echocardiography (a process that used sound waves to show how blood flows through the heart valves) in cardiovascular surgery.

It is amazing how many things you can think of, and the connections you can make between disparate elements of an undertaking, once your mind has been set to roam. It was a joy to only consider the best-case scenarios—instead of always having to fear the worst. The administration was taking a similar approach in every area of the hospital, with the goal of making St. Francis Hospital the leading health-care provider in the metropolitan Hartford area. We would stop at nothing short of offering health-care services whose quality was second to none, with the most modern physical facilities, while at the same time maintaining financial prudence and excellence in our teaching and research efforts.

It was a heady time, marked above all by eliminating the resistance to change. That cleared the way for the open-heart program in particular by providing increased physical space, ancillary services, physicians, and postoperative care, along with publicity. Having come out of the suppressive phase of our open-heart program in my earlier years, this was very refreshing. Instead of responding to letters and fighting for slots, there was now time and focus to shorten the waiting time for our patients. And the numbers bore out our success: In 1989, we performed 900 open-heart procedures—the most ever—and that number was topped again in 1990 when we performed 1,127 adult open-heart surgeries.

We had become the most active adult heart surgery program in Connecticut. As for my relationship with our new CEO, Dr. D'Eramo? He became a friend forever. Just as we started our professional connection seeing eye-to-eye, so we have continued, on both a personal and professional level, to this day.

Chapter Twenty-Two

Prosperity at St. Francis Hospital and Medical Center continued under Dr. D'Eramo for the rest of his eighteen-year tenure, from 1988 to 2006.

In 1990, St. Francis Hospital and its competitor, Mount Sinai, merged which brought back cardiologists, patients for catheterization, and cardiac surgery. A major fundraising event, Miracles, celebrated the merger of the two cultures, and those funds went toward furthering cardiac surgery services.

In January 1991, the hospital received a large donation of more than $2 million from the Maximilian E. & Marion O. Hoffman Foundation. With this funding, we were able to establish the Hoffman Heart and Vascular Institute at St. Francis Hospital, with Dr. Robert Jeresaty as the medical director. This institute provided state-of-the-art diagnostic and intervention technologies, focusing in the areas of prevention, diagnosis, treatments, and rehabilitation. It was staffed by thirty cardiologists and twelve cardiothoracic and vascular surgeons, and it had a full complement of other health-care professionals as well.

This was one of several major pushes by the hospital to promote cardiac surgical services to the next level. Operating-room slots were increased accordingly, and it really looked like the program vision of Planning for the Year 2000 was taking shape. But it was not only the infrastructure that was underway. After all, the outside of the apple may look glossy and perfect, but it is not of value to eat if the inside is rotten. To my mind, Dr. D'Eramo knew this, too, and took pains to address the style and substance of internal communications at the hospital. Through very clear and persuasive letters, he implored members of the administrative staff to take a more active role in providing a direct link between physicians and the offices of individual specialists, such as myself. He urged that such conversations could remain confidential—to do whatever it takes, in other words, to provide superior patient care on every level.

The results truly could not have been more beneficial. The progress of open-heart surgery was now nearing its peak with five cases every day, seven days a week, plus emergency cases. The new chief of surgery at St. Francis, Dr. Robert Painter, was likewise pivotal in promoting cardiac surgery, as were the efforts of Ron LaPensee, the new chief administrative director.

In July of 1994, Dr. Painter wrote:

The Cardiac surgical program has been one of the strongest programs at this Institution, both in terms of quality and generation of substantial amount of income. Since [Dr. D'Eramo] arrived, he has put no limitation on the cardiac program and to ignore any suggestion cardiac surgery is draining the resources of the Institution as we do not believe that is the case."

These were the words we had been waiting so long to hear.

This new period of prosperity for St. Francis Hospital had a great ripple effect in my own life, as it continued to enhance my standing in the professional community. In 1993, upon the recommendation of Dr. Beattie—who was by then working at Beth Israel Medical Center in New York—I was promoted to Associate Clinical Professor at the University of Connecticut. Yes, Dr. Beattie was still around, functioning as my guardian angel. The very same Dr. Beattie who had written the reference for me that allowed me to land my all-important residency with Dr. Najafi all those years ago; the same Dr. Beattie who later provided both a key recommendation letter that got me started in Hartford and a referral to one of my most famous patients, the personal secretary to the president of India. There is no way to repay his beneficence in my life. I could only hope to be a source of such generosity and encouragement to other doctors coming up behind me.

Now in my third decade of practicing medicine, I con-tinued to receive accolades. For several years in a row in the mid-1990s, I was named as one of the best doctors in the State of Connecticut. Being selected as a "best doctor" by my own peers was a huge honor, of course, as it was based not only on the number of cases a physician completed but also the number of high-quality, cutting-edge cases that turned out successfully. One of the accolades they bestowed upon me specifically was saying that I had been instrumental in leading the increase in the number of open-heart surgical cases from 75 per year to 1,200 per year over a twenty-year span (from 1976 to 1996), in conjunction with both the surgical teams and the administration.

It was a little embarrassing to see my face blown up on a billboard advertising my best doctor status! I knew, however, that such publicity could only help the hospital. Many patients, and family members of patients, reported seeing the advertisement when they were driving along I-84 near the hospital.

Of course, such notoriety didn't make me change anything about my routine at work. I continued to take great pains never to get too high or too low with my emotions. I prepared for cases the same way as I always had, studying each one exhaustively the night before the operation as I went through the mental steps of the procedure and prepared myself for any unusual obstacles I might encounter. Only when such a visualization was complete was I able to relax enough to go to sleep.

By 1997, heart surgery at St. Francis topped 1,300 cases a year. It was truly an incredible figure considering we had come from well less than 100 a year. The whole cardiac team, from the nursing staff, operating-room staff, perfusionists, and physician assistants to the anesthesiologists, cardiologists, and all cardiac surgeons, were congratulated by the administration.

Of course, we could not have done it without the administration's enthusiastic support. In retrospect, the history of cardiac surgery at St. Francis Hospital was like constructing a building, beginning with a solid foundation and adding one floor at a time based on excellent patient care. I recalled when we had but a single bed in intensive care, and we were doing one to two cases per week. We still spent countless hours in patient care, training the nursing staff and taking pride in each patient outcome. But in those days, some patients had to wait three to four months for a surgical date.

With the new patient care tower completed, we now had four separate operating rooms dedicated to open-heart surgery, twenty intensive care beds in conjunction with cardiology, and thirty-two stepdown beds. This growth would continue to the point where seven open-heart surgical procedures were allowed per day—whereas we used to have seven per week in 1975: a 400 percent growth!

This rapid expansion in the cardiology and cardiac surgical services would not have been accomplished without the opening of cardiac catheterizations to the private cardiologists and networking with the neighboring communities and hospitals. Nor would it have happened without providing state-of-the-art surgical procedures, from the conventional coronary bypass grafting to advanced mitral valve repairs, thoracoabdominal surgery, and minimal aortic valve surgery procedures. All of this enhanced the visibility of St. Francis Hospital, as did our outcomes, which were similar, if not better than, the national average.

Our main aim then became to solidify our referral base, provide the best care at the least cost to the patient, and work toward early discharge and rehabilitation for every patient. Increased teaching and research, too, brought new technology, which in turn brought safer methods and even more reliable outcomes. St. Francis was on its way to becoming the leading cardiac center in the state of Connecticut.

For my part, when thinking about my contributions to St. Francis's success, the quality I was most proud of was my loyalty. In addition to my manual skills and absolute commitment to the well-being of each patient—as if they themselves were a god, according to my mother's well-remembered injunction—I stayed in one place the entire time. That was the only way I could have been able to contribute to such a success story, and to help steer it in my own way. It was my commitment to that place, to those people. This dedication extended to my whole family as well. Ranjana also played an important role in the hospital, tirelessly dedicating her time and energy to volunteering with the Women's Auxiliary and gift shop to this day. Even my children volunteered in the hospital as teenagers, and later my son took on a full-time role in the communications department! This commitment to the hospital, despite retiring from active practice, continues to this day in manifold ways.

Chapter Twenty-Three

As the future of cardiac surgery at St. Francis was assured, I found myself with more intellectual energy to devote to my special area of interest: mitral valve repairs. I felt less distracted by politics and obstructions and more able to devote myself to making a contribution to the development of medical science in a new way, through invention.

Let me back up. The mitral valve is a small flap that controls the blood flow between the left atrium of the heart and the left ventricle (it is also known as the bicuspid valve). When these flaps don't close tightly, blood leaks backward across the valve. This is called mitral valve regurgitation, and is, in fact, the most common type of heart valve disease. In milder cases, this condition can make the patient feel short of breath. In more serious cases, not enough blood moves through the heart or to the rest of the body, and it can be deadly.

I had been interested in these two leaflets of the mitral valve for many years. In 1987, and again in 1992, I traveled to Paris, where French physicians were lecturing at Le Club Mitrále. In these advanced trainings, we were taught mitral valve repairs rather than the replacement of the mitral valve that had previously been in favor. Dr. Alain Carpentier was our instructor, and he has often been called the father of modern mitral valve repair. He developed and popularized a number of mitral valve repair techniques, concentrating on minimally invasive strategies.

As a result of this eye-opening exposure, I became the resident expert on mitral repair surgery at St. Francis Hospital. Mitral repairs, in fact, became my passion, and St. Francis was on the path to becoming a major mitral valve repair center. I published multiple papers and gave multiple presentations on the topic, discussing both methods of reconstruction and how to know when medications would not be enough and repair would be required.

All this time, I started thinking about how to make mitral valve repair even simpler. If part of the mitral valve was torn, we now knew we didn't have to replace the entire apparatus. That had been the standard procedure, to simply remove a leaky mitral valve. Yet any replacement is always inferior to the original; a new valve can always disintegrate or fatigue. We can never make something for use in the human body that is better than God can make it—that is one of the truisms of medical science. Whenever there is original tissue available for use, that is preferable. Therefore, any invention of mine would have to be made of the toughest and least invasive material possible and be used only for the most limited ends. Since we were no longer simply cutting out the entire valve, might a patch be grafted on top to assist with the repair? Then the body's tissues could naturally grow back on top of the affected area?

I started carrying a piece of paper in my pocket whenever I did my rounds and sketching out what such a device could look like. Everyone at the time said that if you have a good idea—don't disclose it! Someone will steal it from you. So I kept my thoughts to myself, but still they continued.

I chose Gore-Tex for my material because it had been used in a wide variety of medical applications, including sutures and synthetic knee ligaments; it was durable and easy to handle. I was granted a patent for the design of my mitral patch—called MitraPatch—for the first generation in 2006 and the second generation in 2011. I launched my company, Chawla Heart Technologies, LLC. First, however, I would have to get FDA clearance, a laborious process that could sometimes take up to eighteen years! In my case, the process actually moved along a little faster, as there was a similar type of product (a predicate device) in use for another area of the human body. Thus, I was granted permission to skip a few steps.

I had already finished the bench testing—ex vivo experiments, acute and chronic animal model (porcine)—with good results at Emory University in Atlanta with Dr. Muralidhar Padala and Dr. Vinod Thourani. Michele Lucey with Lakeshore MDC Consulting was hired to help with the application and follow up with the FDA. At the time of this writing, we are awaiting the results of chordal tension testing in the human heart at the

University of Arkansas, to be followed by a presentation to the FDA, and hopefully approval.

Throughout my efforts, it was never my desire to seek financial gain from my invention, only to bring the greatest benefit to my patients. This focus served to keep my mind sharp as I turned this intellectual problem over in my mind again and again. By now, I have researched so much about the mitral valve and its possible repair, I could talk about it for hours with scientists and other cardiac surgeons.

Chapter Twenty-Four

The events from 2001 to 2016 could be another book on their own, but I will try to summarize them here. On January 1, 2001, our team of four surgeons and four from the other surgical team united to form the Cardiac & Thoracic Surgical Associates, LLC. I would remain one of the managers, and our new team would superspecialize our surgeons into different fields.

After Dr. D'Eramo departed, Chris Dadlez became the new CEO in October 2004. In May 2005, he offered our group full-time employment, which we declined. However, things were not always harmonious within our group. There was an internal struggle for management. One member retired and another left the team for a hospital in New York. The team was again reorganized in 2007, when Dr. Bill Martinez, Dr. Jack Thayer, and I formed a new group, Cardiothoracic Surgeons PC, which operated until 2016.

As my career reached its apex, I found myself thinking about how I could give back. I had made a series of charitable donations throughout my life, but I sought for some way to combine this work with the legacy of my mother, whose influence I continued to feel keenly throughout my life.

My mother always gave generously in three areas: education, homelessness, and health. I hit upon a solution that would honor at least two of the three of the concerns most dear to my mother's heart. In 1994, there was a new building being erected on the campus of St. Francis. Ranjana and I pledged funds toward the new auditorium, which would be used in part as a medical theater. There were two of my mother's passions, education and health, in one place! I considered the money I earned to have come from God in the first place; it felt right to return some of it. I also found to be true what others have observed about the law of prosperity: The more I gave, the more I made. The money got replenished, in other words.

My contributions earned us the honor of naming rights, so we named the theater the Chawla Auditorium to honor my parents. I was delighted to be able to honor my family in that way, as family has always been of the utmost importance to me.

I can't let a discussion of family continue any longer without celebrating the advice, companionship, and strength I have derived from my marriage to Ranjana—a union that has lasted well over fifty years!

Throughout our entire lives, she has shown remarkable energy and enthusiasm. Ranjana—who had moved to a whole new country and a new life at just twenty-two years old—fit into the community in Rochester immediately. She had a master's degree in psychology and began volunteering her counseling services at the drug clinic at Rochester General Hospital where I worked. When we moved from Rochester to Hartford, she began volunteering at St. Francis, eventually becoming the president of the Women's Auxiliary—not once, but twice! This was in addition to the other nonprofit organizations to which she gave her time, including the Junior League of Hartford, Leadership Greater Hartford, and Riverfront Recapture, an effort to revitalize the banks of the Connecticut River.

Ranjana also made an immeasurable contribution to our family life with the time she devoted to raising our two children. She was a pillar of strength while I worked long hours in the hospital. I tried my best, but it was she who attended to the kids closely while they grew through their academics, activities, and social lives.

In the short period we had to get to know each other before we were married, we did not have the opportunity to talk about our likes and dislikes, whether those attitudes were related to raising a family, or any other topic. Those likes and dislikes take a long time to find out, and we have had occasions when we agreed to disagree. But I always knew how insightful she was and that together we would make a team that was stronger than we could have been on our own individually. As I like to say when reconciling after an argument, "The strength of one and one in a couple with the same ideas and preferences is equal to two, while for a couple with opposite ideas and preferences, their strength is equal to eleven."

As for the two children Ranjana and I have had the privilege and pleasure of raising, they have both brought us immense pride. Our son, Sujit, if you recall, was born during our early days in a Chicago apartment. Over the years, we connected over our shared interests, such as baseball (even though we rooted for different teams!), playing tennis, and cheering on the Hartford Whalers during their glory years. I still have fond memories of our camping weekends during his YMCA Indian Guides (now YMCA Adventure Guides) program. He has made us proud with his accomplishments, including completing a law degree from Widener University and following his passions for arts and entertainment. He continues to engage in marketing the film industry in both the U.S. and India. He has also been involved with helping the underserved with computer classes, with the added benefit that if I need any computer advice, he is always there to help me out, and does so gently! He has grown into a calm, solid, and thoughtful individual who lights up when his nephew and niece enter the room.

Our daughter, Sarika, was born almost four years after her brother, when I had to do my first quadruple bypass surgery. I believe she must have brought good luck to my practice, for, as you will remember, this was immediately after my first patient died on the operating table. This connection has continued throughout our relationship, and I consider her my confidante. One of the wonderful things about Sarika is the way she listens first and does not react, then delivers her viewpoint in a way that easily translates into my future plan of action.

Sarika found her passions through trial and error—playing soccer was not her strength, but reading and writing were! She would even take books to the Hartford Whalers matches while the rest of the family watched the hockey game. She completed her postgraduate work in English literature and creative writing, and she became a published writer and content strategist. She has also given Ranjana and me two beautiful grandchildren, Calvin (thirteen years old at the time of this writing) and Leela (eight years old). Both are adorable and loving like their mother, intelligent, caring, and thoughtful. I hope I can see them grow into their adulthood!

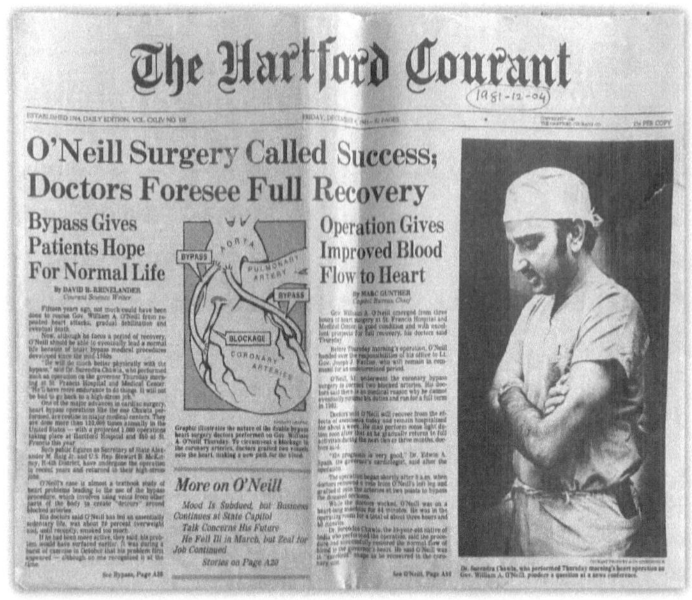

Newspaper article on the successful coronary artery bypass graft of Governor William O'Neill at St. Francis; 1981

Governor O'Neill being discharged from St. Francis Hospital and Medical Center after his operation; 1981

Surendra K. Chawla, M.D.

As a Director of Saint Francis Care, Inc., Dr. Surendra Chawla serves on the Strategic Planning Committee.

Dr. Chawla is the Senior Attending Physician in the Department of Cardiovascular and Thoracic Surgery, and Surgical Director of the Hoffman Heart Institute at Saint Francis Hospital and Medical Center. He has been associated with Saint Francis since 1976.

He is a fellow of the Royal College of Surgeons of Canada by examination both in general surgery and cardiovascular and thoracic surgery. He is a fellow of the American College of Surgeons, and a member of the Society of Thoracic Surgeons, Hartford County Medical Association, Connecticut State Medical Society, and the New England Vascular Society.

Dr. Chawla attended medical school at the All India Institute of Medical Sciences in New Delhi, India. He entered a Master's program in general/cardiac surgery in Chandigarh, India. Dr. Chawla finished his general surgery residency in Rochester General Hospital in Rochester, New York and cardiovascular and thoracic surgery residency at Rush Presbyterian-St. Luke's Medical Center in Chicago, Illinois. Upon completion, he entered private practice in cardiac, thoracic and vascular surgery at Saint Francis.

Dr. Chawla resides in West Hartford with his wife, Ranjana.

My inclusion on the Board of Directors at St. Francis Hospital and Medical Center; 1990

With Dr. David D'Eramo, CEO of St. Francis Hospital and Medical Center, and Archbishop Daniel Cronin; 1990

Receiving the first and only Lifetime Achievement Award along with Dr. Jeresaty from St. Francis Hospital and Medical Center; 2019

DR. SURENDRA K. CHAWLA

Cardiac Surgeons, P.C., Hartford

Surendra Chawla's road to Hartford began "back home" in India, where, when he was about 15, one of his mother's aunts went into a local hospital, "they opened her up, said they couldn't do anything, closed her up, sent her home and she died.

"I remember thinking," says Dr. Chawla, 53, "that maybe something could have been done, and that medicine might not be a bad idea for me—that I could help these kinds of patients." Once he had been chosen for one of 35 medical school openings (out of 5,000 applicants), there followed nine rigorous years of training in New Delhi, then a move halfway across the world. "I knew I wanted to be a cardiac surgeon," he says. "It was a very precise field, and I was good with my hands. But I was not operating back home, so I came to the States to learn the technical side."

Which he did, first as a general surgical resident at Rochester (N.Y.) General Hospital, then as a cardiovascular and thoracic surgical resident at Rush-Presbyterian-St. Luke's Medical Center in Chicago. Since 1976, he has been a private practitioner in Hartford, specializing in cardiac, thoracic and vascular surgery, with St. Francis Hospital and Medical Center his base of operations. Despite multiple commitments—as surgical director of the Hoffman Heart Institute at St. Francis, senior attending in the department of surgery at St. Francis and associate clinical professor in the department of surgery at the University of Connecticut School of Medicine—Chawla is singlemindedly devoted to his patients.

"I care for one patient at a time," he says. "Every one should be taken care of as if he were a relative or a friend. No case is short unless it finishes early. For me the operating room is like a place of worship, and the person lying on the table is a descendant of God. You can't knowingly or unknowingly hurt that patient because you are serving God. I have seen miracles in the operating room. . . I believe there is a supernatural power taking care of that person on the table."

Having cared for patients in Hartford for 20 years now (he operated on former Gov. O'Neill in 1981), Chawla still puts in long days (beginning with hospital rounds at 7:30

a.m. and winding up in his office at 7:30 p.m.), enjoys living in West Hartford, where he and his wife ("the busiest volunteer I've ever known") have raised two children, both now in college, and is satisfied with what he has achieved. "I have reached the pinnacle of whatever I wanted to do," he says. "Now I really enjoy every operation and procedure. I will continue until my hands start to give up.

"But cardiac surgery is here to stay," he adds, noting that while you can exercise daily and control cholesterol, diabetes, smoking, hypertension and obesity, you can't alter your family history, or change from a Type A personality into a Type B.

These immutable facts may help explain why the number of open-heart surgeries at St. Francis Hospital increased from 75 in 1976, the year Chawla arrived on the scene, to 1,200 last year. Another reason may be what Chawla praises as the "excellent patient care and care by nursing services" provided open-heart patients at the hospital. A third is quite possibly the skill and devotion of Chawla himself.

Named one of the Top Doctors in Connecticut Magazine; 1996

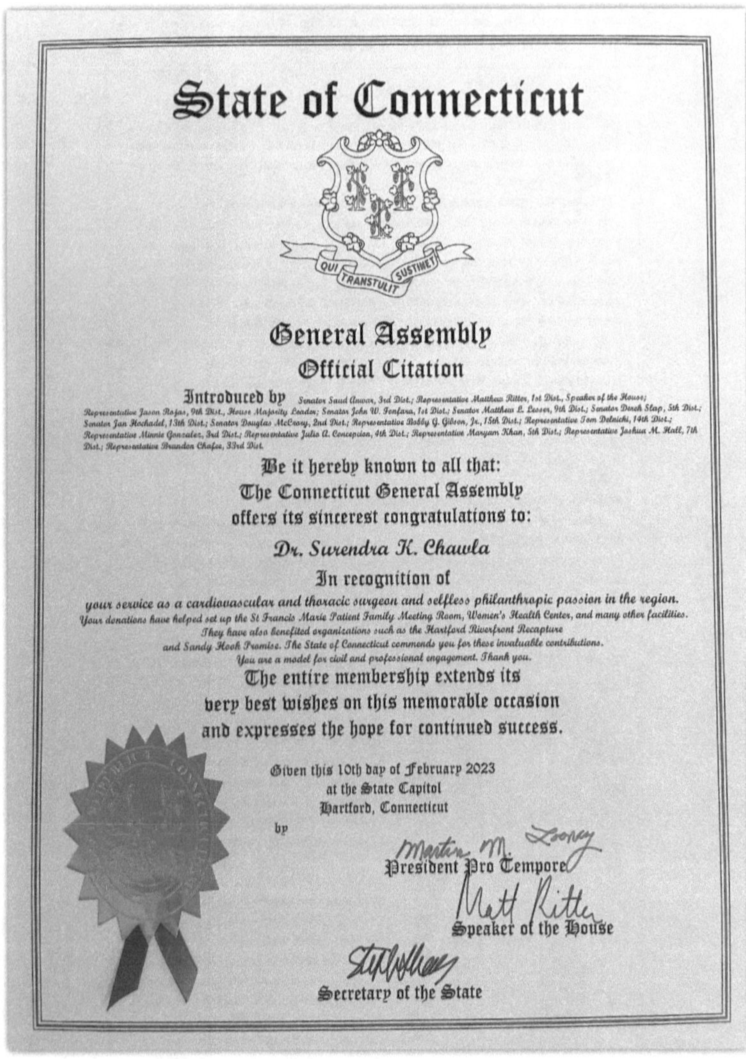

State of Connecticut

General Assembly
Official Citation

Introduced by Senator Saud Anwar, 3rd Dist.; Representative Matthew Ritter, 1st Dist., Speaker of the House; Representative Jason Rojas, 9th Dist., House Majority Leader; Senator John W. Fonfara, 1st Dist.; Senator Matthew L. Lesser, 9th Dist.; Senator Derek Slap, 5th Dist.; Senator Jan Hochadel, 13th Dist.; Senator Douglas McCrory, 2nd Dist.; Representative Bobby G. Gibson, Jr., 15th Dist.; Representative Tom Delnicki, 14th Dist.; Representative Minnie Gonzalez, 3rd Dist.; Representative Julio A. Concepcion, 4th Dist.; Representative Maryam Khan, 5th Dist.; Representative Joshua M. Hall, 7th Dist.; Representative Brandon Chafee, 33rd Dist.

Be it hereby known to all that:
The Connecticut General Assembly
offers its sincerest congratulations to:

Dr. Surendra K. Chawla

In recognition of

your service as a cardiovascular and thoracic surgeon and selfless philanthropic passion in the region.
Your donations have helped set up the St Francis Marie Patient Family Meeting Room, Women's Health Center, and many other facilities.
They have also benefited organizations such as the Hartford Riverfront Recapture
and Sandy Hook Promise. The State of Connecticut commends you for these invaluable contributions.
You are a model for civil and professional engagement. Thank you.

The entire membership extends its
very best wishes on this memorable occasion
and expresses the hope for continued success.

Given this 10th day of February 2023
at the State Capitol
Hartford, Connecticut

by

President Pro Tempore

Speaker of the House

Secretary of the State

General Assembly Official Citation from the State of Connecticut; 2023

The Chawla Auditorium at St. Francis Hospital and Medical Center

At the Chawla Cardiac Surgery Pavilion with Ranjana; 2004

Introducing the Chawla Cardiac Surgery Center at St. Francis Medical Center in *Connecticut Magazine*; 2004

Celebrating the opening of the Vidya Seth Lifelong Learning Center at St. Francis Hospital and Medical Center; 2013

Traveling in Europe with our lifelong friends, Darshan and Manjit Bains

Ranjana and I enjoying time together on a cruise

With our travel crew, the Daltons, Driscolls, Perrettas, and Godars

On my daughter's wedding day, with Sujit, Sarika, and Ranjana

With my great friends, Steve Miller and Howard Case

My dearest grandchildren, Calvin Vikram Rigby and Leela Rigby

Chapter Twenty-Five

I don't think it would ever be easy for someone to retire from a career to which they had devoted their whole mind and heart. Nevertheless, I felt a growing sense that the time for me to step down from active practice might be approaching. I had reached the heights of my profession; the Hoffman Heart and Vascular Institute of Connecticut had even named part of their operation after me, the Chawla Cardiac Surgery Center.

Something else struck me at the same time. I had recently received my physician's practitioner's report. This is where they tell you how many cases you did in the past year and what the result of the work was. I had a perfect score, meaning that whether I was doing a coronary artery bypass graft, mitral valve repair, mitral valve replacement, or aortic valve replacement, I had a zero mortality rate. I could not do any better.

Although I had lived to serve, I was now looking forward to spending more time with my family. All those early mornings when I had to wake up, the night calls and the emergency surgeries—they were taking a toll on my health. I decided to slow down, give up my surgical privileges, and continue as a consultant.

My last night call was on April 2, 2016. I marveled at how far we had come, both in our particular institution and in our medical field in general, that we could help as many people as we did. In my forty years as a surgeon, I performed more than nine thousand cardiac surgeries. It was time to lay my instruments to rest.

By this time, Chris Dadlez had retired, so I presented my personal plans to Dr. John Rodis, who had taken over as the president of St. Francis Hospital that year. I laid out my plans as follows:

1. Reduce my working hours to two days a week for Transcatheter Aortic Valve Replacement, a new start-up clinic.

2. Assist in the operating room as needed.

3. Mentor and promote a new cardiac surgeon, Dr. Sandeep Gupta.

4. Conduct the morbidity and mortality conferences.

5. Start a preventive medicine clinic with Dr. Robert Silverstein.

6. Help the physician assistant program.

7. Help the administration with population health management with Dr. Amit Mody, the administrative vice president.

Dr. Rodis gave the last announcement of relinquishing my surgical privileges:

After performing close to nine thousand open heart cardiac surgical procedures, Dr. Surendra Chawla will be laying his instruments to rest and will lend his unparalleled expertise as a consultant to our first-rate cardiac surgical team.

In this role, effective March 31, 2017, Dr. Chawla's more than forty years of knowledge, innovation, and philanthropy will continue to benefit patients and their families and his colleagues here at St. Francis Hospital and Medical Center. Our medical staff is very fortunate to be able to benefit from Dr. Chawla's knowledge, experience, and expertise in this role model.

We are forever grateful for Dr. Chawla's vision, compassion, and dedication to our hospital and know that we can be assured of his ongoing commitment to our patients and St. Francis Hospital.

A few years after my retirement, I received the first-ever Lifetime Achievement Award, along with Dr. Robert Jeresaty, given by St. Francis Hospital and Medical Center. Along with the kudos I received, the gala at which I received the honor raised millions of dollars for the ongoing work of The Hoffman Heart and Vascular Institute of Connecticut. I left the event that evening knowing that the important work I had contributed to starting will go on long after I am no longer here.

When will that be? One never knows. When my time arrives, it will arrive. As I look back now and scan the events of my past, it is clear that I was destined to live this very life. As a young boy, my entire family was miraculously spared from unimaginable violence during a horrific period in history. In my career, my mentors and colleagues opened up doors for me—they were the people that I was meant to have in my life. My own built-in perseverance (Ranjana may call it stubbornness) never allowed me to give up on my job search. Thanks to a fortunately timed recommendation, I found my way to Hartford, Connecticut—a place I hadn't ever considered—where I spent the next forty-two years building my career at St. Francis Hospital and raising my family alongside my wife.

Every morning, I pray to God for one thing: *God, whatever it is you want me to do, give me the strength to do that work.* For what more could I ask? Providence has already been with me every step of the way.

About the Author

From his earliest days of memorizing pages for his examinations to becoming a prominent cardiac surgeon, Dr Surendra K. Chawla's commitment to learning has never wavered.

Born in Punjab Province of British India, his life took a tumulus turn during the partition of 1947. At only 5 years old, he became part of one of the largest human migrations in history, crossing the newly formed borders between Pakistan and India in the face of horrific violence. Urged at a young age to focus on his education, Dr. Chawla later became part of another powerful immigration story: this time as a talented young physician arriving in the United States in pursuit of unprecedented opportunities.

Dr. Chawla has been recognized for his surgical skills and patient care in the community. He was certified by the American College of Surgeons and Royal College of Surgeons (Canada), both in General and Cardiothoracic Surgery.

As a researcher, he currently holds four patents related to cardiac devices. He has developed the MitraPatch, a mitral valve apparatus repair device that is now under rigorous evaluation by the FDA.

Dr. Chawla has received numerous awards during his career, including a prestigious Lifetime Achievement Award from St. Francis Hospital and Medical Center and a citation from the General Assembly of the State of Connecticut for services as a cardiothoracic surgeon.

At the time of writing, Dr. Chawla was diagnosed with prostate cancer, and is currently undergoing treatment. While he's always been compelled to put his story on paper, it has become more important than ever to explore how his life evolved from past to present.

He and wife, Ranjana, raised their two children, Sujit and Sarika, in the Greater Hartford area. Not only has Dr. Chawla devoted his career to saving countless lives; he and Ranjana are dedicated philanthropists who continue to give back to the community that gave them so much.

Acknowledgments

All of this could not have been achieved without the support of my family. My wife, Ranjana, has been my champion every step of the way. My son, Sujit, is a quiet and thoughtful supporter who is there any time we need him. My daughter, Sarika, has been instrumental in developing this book with her valuable comments throughout the whole process.

Every success in my life has only been possible because of the people who believed in me from the start. When we talk about Providence, it was Dr. Beattie's recommendations that landed me my residency in Chicago and then my job in Hartford—two pivotal moments in my career.

My classmates-turned-colleagues also became my lifelong friends: Dr. Kishan Tandon and Dr. Manjit Bains, and we have had the pleasure of raising our families together and watching our children grow into adults.

I've had the fortune of turning other professional relationships into strong friendships, namely my accountant Howard Case and my attorney Steve Miller.

I would like to thank my nephew, Anurag Chawla, who is my Power of Attorney in India, and was able to keep my concentration on patient care while he was working on my family's social, legal and financial affairs.

There were many supporting specialties who helped our patients, nurses in the OR, critical care, step-down units, respiratory care and rehab personnel. Special thanks to Rose Torromeo, secretary of the Open Heart Unit, who kept the team together like a family.

I would like to give special thanks to Dr. Bimalin "Tosh" Lahiri, Dr. Murthappa Prakash and Dr. Golam Gazi who are always available to help me with my day-to-day health.

Over the years, Ranjana and I made several friends who became our traveling companions: Elaine and Dr. George Dalton, Mary Kay and Thomas Godar, Sheila and Jim Perretta, Janet and Bill Newman, Lori and Bernie Driscoll, Susan and Howard Case, Maureen and Brendon Fox, and Judy and Dave D'Eramo.

Last, but not least, many thanks to my editor, Stuart Horwitz, for listening to my stories and bringing this book to life.